The Duh Awards

05 06 07 08 09 MLT 10 9 8 7 6 5 4 3 2 1

ISBN: 0-7407-5021-6

Library of Congress Control Number: 2004111610

Book design by Lisa Martin
Illustrations by Matt Taylor

The Duh Awards

In This Stupid World, We Take the Prize

Bob Fenster

**Andrews McMeel
Publishing**

Kansas City

Contents

Introduction

The Russian writer Tolstoy once called upon an aristocrat to demonstrate humility by traveling second class on a train. The nobleman agreed. The next time he took a train, he rented an entire second-class car for himself.

That's a winner, I thought. Or would be if anyone gave prizes for all the crazy, stupid moments that make up so much of our lives from day to day. But they don't.

Do we really need more prizes for the rich, the bright, the beautiful? They're already winners.

And if the supply of awards for the top people runs low, they simply make up some new ones and give them to themselves.

"Won again? What a surprise!"

"You're doing a superb job," they tell each other. "Here, have a raise and another of these cute, little trophies."

But aren't most big shots secretly like movie producer Joseph Levine, who explained the key to success: "You can fool all the people all the time if the advertising is right and the budget is big enough."

What about the stupid, the strange, the losers? Who rewards them for their efforts to make our world the Absurdity Capital of the mid-galaxy area?

Dustin Hoffman may win the Oscar for *Rain Man*. But what about comedy writer Larry Gelbart, who had to work with Hoffman when writing *Tootsie*? Doesn't Gelbart deserve an Anti-Oscar for Best Performance in a Snit when he points out, "My experience with Hoffman taught me one lesson of immense value: Never work with an Oscar winner who is shorter than the statue."

Barry Bonds may win the Most Valuable Unliked Player Award, but what about Edward Bennett Williams? Doesn't he deserve the Most Valuable Did He Really Say That Award?

Williams was a lawyer who once owned the Washington Redskins football team and the Baltimore Orioles baseball team—so he knew what he was talking about when he said, "The only thing dumber than a dumb football owner is a smart baseball owner."

And the only thing dumber than life's losers are life's winners. That's what this book is all about—the long-awaited awards for the weird winners, the dumb losers, and the rest of us.

☆ **PART ONE** ☆

Chapter 1

Boss of the Year
and Other Slave Driver Awards

Alexander the Great was leading his army across the desert, but they were running out of water, about to die of thirst. One of his soldiers offered Alexander the last of the water. The general took that water and poured it into the sand.

"If my men don't drink," he said, "I don't drink."

And that's why they called him Alexander the Great, not Alexander the So-So.

Have you ever had a boss like that? Me neither.

The bosses I've worked for would have stayed on the safe side of the desert and sent their people across, saying, "Guys, if you make it to the other side, send word. Oh, and you'd better leave those canteens with me. They'd only weigh you down."

Which brings us around to the winners of the Boss of the Year Awards.

THE SLAVE DRIVER AWARDS:
RECOGNIZING INNOVATIONS IN MANAGEMENT
THAT WOULD MAKE CAPTAIN QUEEG PROUD

★ **Third Place:** The Word Boss

James Gordon Bennett, Jr., a fussy newspaper publisher and editor of the *New York Herald*, insisted that all his reporters use the word "night" in their stories instead of "evening."

"Night," he explained, "is a more exact term."

Bennett was finally shown the error of his minor tyranny when a reporter filed a story about a society woman who "looked ravishing in a pink silk night gown."

★ **Runner-up:** The Lawn Boss

Generoso Pope, Jr., who turned the *National Enquirer* into America's most successful weekly tabloid, reportedly measured the grass on the company lawn with a ruler to make sure it was cut precisely three inches high.

★ **And the Winner Is:** The Star Exec

Studio executives at Warner Brothers inserted a clause in movie star Bette Davis's contract that she had to make an appearance at the Republican National Convention—even though Davis was a registered Democrat.

Bette's contract also prevented the star from getting divorced for three years unless the studio gave its permission.

THE OVERTIME PRIZE: GOES TO NAPOLEON

To keep the army and the rest of the French empire humming, Napoleon often worked all day and night, and insisted that his staff keep up with his punishing work schedule.

One of his assistants said in admiration, "God made Bonaparte, then rested."

Another assistant replied in exhaustion, "God should have rested a little earlier."

THE BOSSY BOSS AWARDS:
FOR MOVES ONLY A BOSS COULD MAKE WITHOUT GETTING FIRED

We look at our boss and think: He's making a hundred times what I make—he must know something.

What the boss knows is this secret: he doesn't deserve it any more than you do. He gets it because he can give it to himself.

Think of your boss as the manager of a last-place baseball team. He can no longer hit the long ball, if he ever could. He cannot strike anyone out, if he ever could. He can't run the bases even if death were on his heels, which it probably is. He has only one power left. He gets to say who plays and who has to sit on the bench.

★ **Third Place:** The Principled Principal
In 1997 an Alabama high school principal made an executive decision to cancel the school prom. Why? To prevent interracial couples from attending. He didn't want them to have a night to remember.

Later, he had a night to remember when the school was set on fire.

★ **Runner-up:** The Principled Researcher
In the 1970s Dr. Landrum Shettles did pioneering research in the

field of in vitro fertilization while working at Columbia University's medical school.

But the head of his research group was morally outraged that Shettles was trying to create the first test-tube baby. The boss destroyed the experiment by opening sealed containers so the women's eggs couldn't be implanted.

The research continued anyway. Some one hundred thousand babies have been born through in vitro in the United States alone.

★ **And the Winner Is:** The Station Manager

In 1993 a guard at a TV station in Tulsa, Oklahoma, helped a woman whose car wouldn't start by letting her inside to use the phone. Once inside, she pulled a gun on the guard and let in an accomplice. They proceeded to rob the place.

Or did they?

Turns out the robbery was a test dreamed up by the boss to see how employees would react. With bosses like that, you can't afford enemies.

THE BOOT THAT CAN'T BE LICKED TROPHY

Before Lyndon Johnson became a Texas senator and eventually president, he was the tough head of a government agency. Passing a worker's cluttered desk, he scolded the man, saying, "I hope your mind's not as messy as that desk."

Trying to keep on the good side of his boss, the worker immediately cleaned off his desk. But the next time Johnson came through the office, he said to the same man, "I hope your mind's not as empty as that desk."

GREAT MOMENTS ON THE FIRING LINE OF THE CORPORATE LAY-OFF WARS

You have to admire the courage of corporate execs who say they hate to lay people off—then do it anyway. Firing people makes them feel so bad, only huge bonuses can console them.

But faced with layoffs during economic downturns, bosses don't lose their competitive edge. They double their efforts to find creative ways to make dumping people look like something the dumpees should thank them for.

Here are heroic bosses and companies who led the way in the firing game—and one lone employee who topped them all with a brief moment of revenge:

1. When he was a Broadway producer, George M. Cohan fired a young actor from one of his shows because he had no romantic appeal. Who was the dumped actor? Clark Gable, who went on to become one of the most romantic of Hollywood's leading men.

2. National Semiconductor didn't lay off workers. It "reshaped" the company (presumably firing only those workers who were stubbornly out of shape).

3. Xerox found itself faced with "involuntary force reductions." As in, don't blame me for firing you, Jones, I did it involuntarily.

No doubt when company execs managed to salvage millions for their own profit-taking, that was voluntary.

4. The once and future great New York Yankees sank to the bottom of the baseball world in 1966. Their fans decided not to sink with them and stayed away in droves.

So when Yankee TV announcer Red Barber had his cameraman pan the stands during a particularly woeful game, his bosses were not amused. Why? There were fewer than five hundred people in the stadium.

Barber, who had been the Yankee man on radio and TV for thirty-four years, was fired.

5. Modern corporations could learn a few tricks in the art of laying people off from the ancient Romans.

It was considered a great honor for a girl to be chosen as a vestal virgin at a Roman temple. But if she lost her virginity while in service, she was laid both off and down. She wasn't just let go—she was buried alive.

Can't you hear the wheels turning down at corporate HQ?

6. On the home front of the firing line, movie star Gloria Swanson went through an endless series of maids and cooks. Any time they cooked or cleaned, she went over their work herself and did it better. She fired them all when she should have fired only one person—herself.

7. Jimmy Breslin, the crusading New York City newspaper columnist, became a hero to working stiffs everywhere as one of the few people to fire his boss.

In 1986–87 Breslin hosted a late-night TV show called *Jimmy Breslin's People*. But he got fed up with the way ABC handled the show. Instead of quitting, he fired the network.

Breslin took out a full-page ad in the *New York Times* to let his bosses know: "ABC, your services, such as they are, will no longer be required."

THE HOLLYWOOD PERK AWARD

When Jack Warner ran Warner Brothers studio, he had an assistant follow him into the bathroom so he didn't have to flush his own toilet.

THE LEADERSHIP AWARDS:
FOR BOSSES WITH UNIQUE VISION

★ **Third Place:** The Crusading Publisher

In the late 1800s an English publisher took over the *Chicago Tribune* newspaper and began a campaign to get fireworks banned at Fourth of July celebrations. Why? The firecrackers frightened his young daughter.

★ **Runner-up:** Captain of the Border Guards

Mexican painter José Orozco had the odd habit of destroying his own paintings if they displeased him, even after he became popular enough to sell anything with his name on it.

When Orozco traveled to the United States in 1917 to set up a big show, the head customs official in Laredo, Texas, ordered that sixty of his paintings be destroyed, explaining that it was illegal to bring "immoral" pictures into the country.

Orozco could have made a fortune from the paintings that were burned. Or if that customs officer had been smart enough to confiscate the canvases instead of burning them, maybe he would have made that fortune.

★ **And the Winner Is:** The Boss of Bosses

According to journalist Dick Schaap, when he wrote a biography of Yankee owner George Steinbrenner, the Boss offered to buy every copy of the first edition if Schaap would make the changes Steinbrenner wanted for the second edition.

Schaap turned him down—thereby cutting off a windfall industry for writers—authoring nasty biographies of famous people and selling the results to the subjects of the books.

THE JUST-FOLLOWING-ORDERS AWARD

As head of the FBI, J. Edgar Hoover ruled the agency with a picky hand. When he disapproved of the manner in which an agent had written a memo—with the words typed too close to the edge of the page—Hoover scribbled a note and sent the memo back. The note instructed the agent to "watch the borders."

The agent showed Hoover's note to his supervisor, and FBI agents were immediately pulled off other assignments and sent to man the borders between the United States and Mexico.

THE ENLIGHTENED EMPLOYERS AWARD: HONORING KID-FRIENDLY INDUSTRIES

★ **Third Place:** The Factories
In 1833 England passed a child-protection law making it illegal for factory owners to force their nine-year-old employees to work longer than nine hours a day.

★ **Runner-up:** The Mines
In 1842 England passed a law that prohibited coal companies from hiring miners under the age of ten. Prior to this law, kids as young as three worked inside the coal mines because they could crawl through passages too tight for older child miners.

★ **And the Winner Is:** The Mill
Children were forced to work as machine operators even though they were young, orphans most of them. They had to sleep three

in a bed on straw that was changed only once a month, wearing clothes that were washed only twice a month. For this, the kids said, "Thank you, sir, may I have another?"

These working conditions were considered as good as they got back in the 1800s when Scottish textile manufacturer and social reformer Robert Owen improved working conditions for children at his mill.

Owen was considered a hero by the orphans. If he hadn't put them to work in his factory, the kids faced an even bleaker life of crime, starvation, or drudgery in other industries not so enlightened.

THE HMM, THAT ACTUALLY MIGHT WORK TROPHY:
FOR GOOD MANAGEMENT IDEAS, AS RARE AS THEY MAY BE

★ **Third Place:** Not a Single Room

In 2003 the Boston Red Sox and their arch rivals, the New York Yankees, were trying to sign free agent pitcher Jose Contreras. The Sox management rented all the rooms in the hotel in which Contreras was staying so Yankee officials could not get close to him.

Despite that clever strategy, the Yankees thwarted the Sox and signed him anyway.

★ **Runner-up:** The Perfect Design

Writer and artist Gelett Burgess invented the Nonsense Machine, designed to do absolutely nothing but with 100 percent efficiency.

★ **And the Winner Is:** Out of the Office

Auto tycoon Henry Ford did not summon his managers into his own office for consultations. Instead, he went to their offices.

Why? "I've found that I can leave the other fellow's office a lot quicker than I can get him to leave mine," Ford explained.

THE HIGH-TECH REVOLUTION AWARD

★ **Third Place:** Modernizing the Workplace

When Andy Grove ran Intel, an assistant was assigned to the task of making sure that everyone who showed up for work after eight in the morning signed the company's Late List.

★ **Runner-up:** Handling the Competition

The engineer William Shockley revolutionized technology by developing the first transistors in 1956. But he treated the engineers who worked for him miserably—insisting they take polygraph tests, refusing to share vital information with them.

Fed up with the boss, many of his staff left to form other technology companies. Shockley had created his own competition.

★ **And the Winner Is:** Staying in Touch with a Changing World

Executives in American corporations were asked to complete a survey to test their pop culture awareness. Nearly half of them thought Fiona Apple was a new computer model.

The same question was asked of sixth grade students, and 90 percent of them knew she was a pop singer.

THE PAPA BOSS AWARD

When movie star Robert Taylor was under contract to MGM, he asked the studio boss, Louis B. Mayer, for a raise.

Instead of giving him more money, Mayer said, "If God had given me a son, I would want him to be exactly like you. It hurts me deeply that you've asked for money at a time like this."

When a friend asked Taylor if he'd gotten his raise, the actor said, "No, but I got a father."

Chapter 2

Twenty-Four-Karat-Gold Medals:
The Rich Go for the Gold

If you're *not* one of the 447 richest people in the world, here's where you stand: Take half the working people in the world. Add up all the money they make in a year. The 447 richest make more.

Yes, the rich do have all the money that by rights you and I should have. Well, me anyway. But what the wealthy don't have is the love and understanding of the common people. They're pretty sure they don't need it, but if it turns out they do they'll send someone out to buy some.

Meanwhile, the wealthy will have to make do with the twenty-four-karat-gold medals, the awards for people too rich to need awards.

In this contest, their Golden Touch (the ability to make money no matter how loony they are) brings them a sweep of the first-place ribbons. They'd probably take the second- and third-place prizes too, but don't want to clutter up their mantels with the tackier ribbons if they don't match the drapes.

FIRST PLACE IN EXPECTORATIONS

How are the rich different than you and me? In every conceivable way. Even their spit is worth more than ours.

Hollywood talent manager Bernie Brillstein reflected on the time he sold his movie company for $26.5 million. He commented that at today's inflated values that price was: "just spit. But then it was a lot of money."

FIRST PLACE IN GOLD PLATING

Millionaire "Diamond" Jim Brady mastered the art of big spending, but didn't know much about bicycles. In the 1920s he gave singer Lillian Russell a bike dipped in gold and smothered with hundreds of emeralds, sapphires, rubies, and, of course, diamonds.

Brady suggested that the singer take the bike out for a spin through Manhattan. Police squads had to rescue her from a crowd that tried to rip the bike to pieces.

FIRST PLACE IN SAVING MONEY

Ty Cobb may have been the meanest man ever to play baseball. But he was also a mean businessman who became rich from his investments after retiring from the game. Cobb was so cheap that as he lay on his deathbed in 1961, he ordered all the lights in his mansion turned off to save money.

What was he saving it for?

FIRST PLACE IN NOT SAVING MONEY

Before he became a movie star, comic W. C. Fields toured the country in vaudeville. To make sure he didn't lose the money he made on the road, Fields opened small bank accounts in the towns he played along the way.

Eventually, he had seven hundred of these small accounts but forgot where they were, losing over $1 million (at a time when $1 million meant something) because he couldn't remember where he put it.

FIRST PLACE IN FAILING UP

If you've got the Golden Touch, the rewards of failure are just about as profitable as the rewards of success.

Michael Ovitz was the most powerful agent in Hollywood when he left Creative Artists Agency to work for Disney as the studio's number-two boss.

It took a year for Ovitz to realize he didn't like being second to anyone and for Disney to realize that Ovitz wasn't worth what they were paying him.

How much did the studio pay Ovitz to hit the road? Severance pay of $90 million. Imagine what Hollywood pays for someone who gets the job done.

FIRST PLACE IN BABY-SITTING

When King Louis XIV was born in 1638, he was assigned seventeen servants.

As infants, most of us are forced to get by with three or four. Even a parent or two will suffice if we can't afford better help.

But you can hardly expect a royal baby to manage his affairs with only sixteen servants, do you?

FIRST PLACE IN CHILD CARE

President William Howard Taft had an original explanation as to why he spoiled his young children with expensive gifts. "I figure if I give them every luxury now, they won't be spoiled by it later on."

FIRST PLACE IN EMPLOYEE RELATIONS

In ancient Egypt owning gold was a privilege of royalty. But before the ruling class could amuse themselves by covering everything in gold (including each other), it had to be dug out of the mines of Egypt and Nubia.

This was tough, dangerous work. Gold slaves were killed by cave-ins, heat and oxygen depletion, or the arsenic released from rocks by mining for gold.

If the slaves survived those hazards, they earned the right to be worked to death in the mines, then tossed aside and replaced by more ill-fated slaves.

For rulers of ancient civilization, this was what other people were for—to be turned into slaves and tossed aside. Primitive people may have dabbled in slavery too, but never in a businesslike manner. Civilization may be seen as the cost-effective organization of tough luck.

FIRST PLACE IN PERKS

Beau Brummell, the English style setter, had only a small fortune, but a vast sense of style. He had his shoes polished daily with champagne.

FIRST PLACE IN ORCHESTRA SEATS

Isaac Singer made a fortune selling sewing machines in the 1800s. Under the theory that if you flaunt it, you must have it, Singer also made significant advances in the field of turning Type A behavior into A-plus behavior.

He ordered a two-ton carriage built that seated thirty-one people plus a small orchestra.

The carriage required nine horses to pull it down the streets of Manhattan, which weren't quite as jammed with traffic then as they are now—unless Singer's carriage rolled by.

FIRST PLACE IN NEIGHBORS

"It is the wretchedness of being rich," the critic Logan Pearsall Smith said, "that you have to live with rich people."

FIRST PLACE IN MONEY MANAGEMENT

Governments believe that you can waste as much money as you like if you can always print up more.

While plenty of us have the talent to waste a great fortune, we simply don't have the money to get the job done.

Still, seeing all that glitters doesn't mean you can hold on to it even when it is gold. During the 1500s the Spanish conquistadores looted South America, stealing millions of dollars' worth of gold from the Incas and shipping it back to Spain.

Despite one of the largest thefts in history, Spain was so badly managed by its king and the ruling class that the country actually lost money on the deal—spending so excessively, investing so foolishly, that Spain came out of this gold rush poorer than it went in.

FIRST PLACE IN FIRST-CLASS
SPIRITUAL TRANSCENDENCE

Fleetwood Mac's cofounder, Mick Fleetwood, went bankrupt even though the band sold millions of albums.

"Oh my God, I've managed to lose $8 million," he said. "But I've never been terribly attached to material things."

If you or I had $8 million to throw away, maybe we wouldn't be so terribly attached either.

FIRST PLACE IN RELIGIOUS ENLIGHTENMENT

When El Salvadoran priests tried to help the nation's numerous poor, many of their wealthy countrymen responded by leaving the Catholic Church.

They formed a new church that preached God was on the side of the rich, which is why He punished poor people by making them poor.

Or as Jesus said: Love thy neighbor as thyself as long as he's in the same country club as you are.

FIRST PLACE IN FAN SATISFACTION

The English rock band, the Who, broke new ground in the arena of live performances when they smashed up their own equipment at the end of a concert in 1964.

What began as a spontaneous outburst of rock passion quickly became a routine part of their act, as their fans demanded destruction with their music.

The Who were forced to spend over half a million dollars replacing smashed instruments.

FIRST PLACE IN DOORBELLS

Henry Flagler, one of Florida's richest land developers, had neither bell nor knocker on the front door of his Palm Beach estate. Instead, he employed two uniformed doormen to stand outside the house and save visitors the discomfort of ringing the bell.

FIRST PLACE IN NOTHING

Nicolas Cage agreed to take *only* $250,000 for starring in *Leaving Las Vegas*, the offbeat movie about an alcoholic. The general wisdom in Hollywood was that Cage sacrificed real money for a shot at winning an Oscar in a serious film.

"Doing something good never hurt anyone," talent manager Bernie Brillstein explained, "even if you get no money for it."

How many of us could manage to get by on that $250,000 for a few months' work?

FIRST PLACE IN THE FAMILY

Alfred Du Pont scandalized his wealthy family by marrying his second cousin in 1907. Miffed by their criticism, he erected a nine-foot wall around his three-hundred-acre estate in Delaware so he could "keep out intruders," he explained, "mainly of the name Du Pont."

FIRST PLACE IN CAMEOS

Sports fans complain that spoiled athletes are overpaid and they are. But that's nothing compared to how much spoiled movie stars are overpaid.

As a top Hollywood star, you make as much for three months of work on a movie production as baseball's top sluggers make for a three-year contract. Plus, there's no one throwing a major league curve at a movie star. If they did, the studio would bring in a stunt man to face it.

Or as movie director Billy Wilder put it, "Marlon Brando got, for an aggregate of twenty minutes on the screen in *Superman* and *Apocalypse Now*, more money than Clark Gable got for twenty years at MGM."

FIRST PLACE AT DINNER

"The best number for a dinner party is two," British oil tycoon Nubar Gulbenkian said, "myself and a damn good headwaiter."

FIRST PLACE IN MYSTERY

"Architects give us temples in which something marvelous is obviously going on," writer Kurt Vonnegut reasoned. "Actually, practically nothing is going on."

FIRST PLACE IN DELEGATING

Jon Peters was one of the most powerful men in Hollywood when he ran Columbia Studios. All business, he had his driver phone ahead to the studio each morning so a guard could open the front door of the executive building as his limo pulled up.

A second studio employee had an even more important function: He was stationed in the lobby, and it was his job to push the button on Peters's private elevator.

First Place in Hogs

Members of the Guggenheim Motorcycle Club are not your typical bikers. They're all motorcycle-riding movie stars and other millionaires.

Do they ride their Hogs into Palm Springs and have their agents terrorize the natives while they sip Perrier? Not exactly. Club members fly their bikes around the globe looking for unusual places to ride.

First Place in Impossibleness

Movie mogul Barry Diller commented on the abrasive leadership style of movie mogul Jon Peters: "Jon's an impossible person, but his impossibleness is somewhat lovable."

How much impossibleness did he get away with? Steve Roth was supposed to be the producer of one of Arnold Schwarzenegger's lesser efforts, *Last Action Hero*. When Peters and the other studio bosses decided to head the production themselves, they paid Roth $1 million to do nothing.

Most of us would have been willing to do nothing for fifty, sixty grand.

First Place in Advice

William Knudsen, head of General Motors, offered this advice on the ways of wealth: "When a man with money meets a man with experience, the man with the experience gets the money and the man with the money gets the experience."

So Close, Yet So Far Away Awards:
For people who could have become rich, rich, rich but instead sold out as quickly as they could

★ **Third Place:** This Little Pin?

Inventor Walter Hunt patented the first safety pin in 1849. Could have made millions off what became a common household aid. But he was $15 in debt at the time, needed cash, and sold the rights to the safety pin for $400.

★ **Runner-up:** How About Pretty Good Man?

The two comic book artists who created Superman, Joe Shuster and Jerry Siegel, sold the rights to D.C. Comics for a few hundred dollars in 1938.

Superman went on to make millions for the comic book publisher, TV producers, and moviemakers. But not for the guys who created the Man of Steel. They were fired when they asked for a raise.

In 1978 one of the movie studios cashing in on Superman films was finally guilted into paying the Super creators a decent amount of money. By then it was forty years too late. The artists were old men.

★ **And the Winner Is:** Thanks for the Suggestion

Happier ending time—though still not as happy as it should have been.

A teenage sales clerk at a Sears store in Massachusetts dropped an idea into the suggestion box for a new snap-release socket wrench. Sears offered him $10,000 for the rights to the patent in 1964. The wrench went on to sell millions.

The inventor had to take the company to court, claiming Sears execs knew all along they had a big seller on their hands. He finally won $1 million in back royalties.

THE TRICKLE-DOWN PRIZES: FOR EVERYDAY THINGS
THAT WERE ONCE THE EXCLUSIVE PROVINCE OF THE RICH

Who said the rich never gave us anything besides their tax bills? Many of the things we consider everyday commodities were once the exclusive privilege of the nose-up crowd.

★ **Third Place:** Ice

For hundreds of years, ice, in nonicy areas, was a luxury of the rich. Only the wealthy could afford to build underground ice-houses, where large blocks of ice were stored to melt slowly over a hot summer.

In the 1800s improvements in insulation and transportation led to lower prices for pond ice, which became a treat for the less affluent.

★ **Runner-up:** Lemonade

The drink of the rich—that's what lemonade was in the seventeenth century because lemons had to be imported from the Mediterranean and sugar from the West Indies—and both were expensive.

Once lemons and sugar became plentiful, the rich stopped drinking lemonade and the poor took over.

★ **And the Winner Is:** Chips

Potato chips, snack food for the masses, were invented by a resort chef in Saratoga Springs in 1853 when one of the wealthy guests complained that the potatoes served with dinner were too thick. The chef cut potatoes as thin as possible and fried them up exclusively for the resort guest.

Saratoga Chips became a food craze among the wealthy, served on fine china and silver platters only in the best restaurants. By the time potato chips reached the average snacker, they were served cold out of a bag.

GREAT MOMENTS OF THE IDLE RICH

1. French playwright Jean Anouilh—"Every man thinks God is on his side. The rich and powerful know he is."

2. English writer Martin Amis—"Whether or not you've made the stuff yourself, you have to set about pretending that you merit it, that money chose right in choosing you, and that you'll do right by money in your turn."

3. Bodybuilder, film star, and California governor Arnold Schwarzenegger: "Money doesn't make you happy. I now have $50 million, but I was just as happy when I had $48 million."

4. Comedian Joe E. Lewis—"It doesn't matter if you're rich or poor, as long as you've got money."

5. Lawyer William Travers observed during a Newport yacht race that all the boats were owned by rich stockbrokers. "And where are the customers' yachts?" he asked.

6. British writer Malcolm Muggeridge—"People always loathe the rich and powerful. The difference seems to be that in the nineteenth century the English liked being loathed, whereas it appears that Americans rather dislike it."

7. Writer Paul Erdman—"The entire essence of America is the hope to first make money, then make money with money, then make lots of money with lots of money."

8. Novelist Christina Stead—"If all the rich men in the world divided up their money amongst themselves, there wouldn't be enough to go around."

9. Media mogul Robert Sarnoff—"Finance is the art of passing currency from hand to hand until it finally disappears."

THE TRICKLE-UP PRIZE

In the sixteenth century, butter and oysters—now recognized as gourmet essentials in French cuisine—were so common and ill-thought of that they were abhorred by the elite of France and fed only to the poor.

Chapter 3

The Know-a-Little, Talk-a-Lot Society Presents the Anti-Expert Awards

If it wasn't for experts who get it wrong, there goes TV news. In attempting to turn news into entertainment, TV news shows line up enough pundits so that every possibility can be predicted. That way, if most of the experts get it wrong, someone is bound to get it right.

Much of recorded history is incorrectly recorded—which gives subsequent authorities the chance to sound smart by correcting them.

The Anti-Expert Awards honor every authority who said the sky was falling when it wasn't, or that it wasn't when it was.

The Hollywood Vision Award:
For people who can explain why we all still enjoy silent movies so much

★ **Third Place:** Movie Camera Developer Thomas Edison

"I have determined that there's no market for talking pictures," Edison declared in 1926.

★ **Runner-up:** Movie Director D. W. Griffith

That same year, Griffith assured Hollywood, "Speaking movies are impossible. When a century has passed, all thought of our so-called talking pictures will have been abandoned."

★ **And the Winner Is:** Silent Screen Star Mary Pickford

In 1925 the smartest and most successful woman in Hollywood scoffed, "Adding sound to movies would be like putting lipstick on the Venus de Milo."

Venus in lipstick? Good idea, Mary. Make up!

The Magazine Publishers Clear the House Medal:
Goes to the magazine that hardly ever tells its readers to walk off a cliff

Each issue of *Trail* magazine contains maps and directions for great hikes all over the British Isles. Most of them don't lead hikers off a cliff. But the February edition of 2004 did.

If you followed the magazine's directions up the tallest mountain in Great Britain, Ben Nevis, you might enjoy the view. And if the sky was clear enough, you might figure out that the next set of directions took you directly off a cliff more than four thousand feet high. If the fog was heavy, you'd find out soon enough.

The magazine's editor apologized to readers and assured them that it was not a change in editorial policy to send its readers off the deep end.

THE INVENTION PREVENTION AWARD:
FOR EXPERTS WHO KNOW A BAD IDEA WHEN THEY SEE IT

★ **Third Place:** People Cannot Fly

English engineer Frederick Lanchester was an aeronautical pioneer who established the principles of flight in the early 1900s, before the Wright Brothers came to the same conclusions from their own research.

When Lanchester presented his original ideas to English scientific societies, they were rejected. The other scientists thought his curious notions would never lead to successful flight.

The experts were so convincing (you know how intelligent that English accent sounds) that Lanchester gave up his high flying pursuits and moved on to other studies, none of which led to anything as amazing as the airplane.

★ **Runner-up:** It'll Never Replace Carbon Paper

The photocopier was invented in 1938 by Chester Carlson of New York City. But manufacturers rejected his idea, predicting there was no money to be made in copy machines. After all, carbon paper was handling the job of making copies, and that was good enough.

It took Carlson twenty years to develop a working machine and make a fortune for the eventual manufacturer, Xerox.

There was a curious side effect with the introduction of the copy machine into every office, government, or business. "Once the Xerox copier was invented," U.N. ambassador Andrew Young said, "diplomacy died."

★ **And the Winner Is:** The Handyman's Bench that No One Will Ever Buy

Ronald Hickman, a designer for Lotus cars, invented the Workmate portable workbench for do-it-yourselfers. Simple concept—a foldable work table for home-repair projects. Should have been an obvious success.

But hardware companies rejected his idea, explaining that few people would buy one. One manufacturer said Hickman would be lucky to sell a few dozen workbenches.

When Black & Decker finally agreed to manufacture the bench, the company sold 55 million of them.

THE STANDARD PRIZE: FOR INSTITUTIONS
THAT MAINTAIN HIGH STANDARDS OF SNOOTINESS

The *New York Times* proclaimed Webster's Third International Dictionary deficient in 1961. Editors announced to readers that the newspaper would use only the older Second International Dictionary to make usage judgments.

A linguist read through the issue of the Times that contained that pronouncement and discovered nineteen words prohibited by the Second International.

THE THANKS BUT NO THANKS AWARD: FOR PEOPLE WHO
LOOKED AMAZING OPPORTUNITY IN THE FACE AND PASSED

★ **Third Place:** The Unsung Song

The song was first offered to soul singer Sam Cooke. But the singer's manager threw it in the trash because he knew a loser when he heard one.

Someone from the record label picked it out of the trash and gave it to pop star Ricky Nelson, who turned it into a number-one hit: "Travelin' Man."

★ **Runner-up:** I Can See It Now—Fish!

When Clarence Birdseye invented a quick-freezing method for food in 1927, he used it to freeze fish, not veggies. His company quickly went bankrupt.

But when Birdseye sold out to the Postum Company, the cereal manufacturer realized that people wanted a lot of frozen vegetables, not a lot of fish. Birdseye became one of the most familiar products in American homes, but without Clarence Birdseye.

★ **And the Winner Is:** Thirty-five Dollars and the Whole Thing Is Yours

Jell-O was invented in 1845 by Peter Cooper, who spent most of his workshop time tinkering with trains. He was so busy with his trains that he put his instant gelatin idea on a back shelf and never did anything with it.

Jell-O was reinvented fifty years later and patented by a New Yorker named Pearl Wait, who tried to sell it door to door. That approach didn't work either.

Wait's Jell-O was such a flop that he sold the company for a few hundred dollars to Orator Woodward, who was already in the food business. But Woodward couldn't make a go of Jell-O either. In 1899 he offered rights to the product to one of his employees for $35.

He was turned down.

By 1906 Woodward's company was selling $1 million worth of Jell-O a year. Little more was heard from the guy who could have had all that for only $35.

THE DEAF EAR TURNED PRIZE:
GOES TO THE WOMAN WHO DIDN'T LISTEN TO ADVICE

Literary critics in the 1930s told would-be writer Ellen Glasgow to stop writing. As one male critic informed her, "The greatest woman is not the woman who has written the finest book but the woman who has had the finest babies."

Ignoring that advice, Glasgow wrote the novel *In This Our Life*, which won the Pulitzer Prize in 1942.

THE BIG MOUTH PRIZE: FOR PEOPLE WHO
SHOULD HAVE KEPT THEIR SHOES ON THE GROUND

★ **Third Place:** Your Shrinking Computer

In 1949 Popular Mechanics magazine looked at the future of computers and saw the machines shrinking. Editors declared, "Computers in the future may weigh no more than 1.5 tons."

★ **Runner-up:** Smarter People

In 1892 Charles Eliot said, "We find on every hand evidence of the increasing intelligence in large masses of people."

Eliot was president of Harvard University at the time he made that proclamation. Large masses of people never went near Harvard and still don't.

In the twentieth century, those smart masses managed to kill 60 million people in wars. If the masses get any smarter in the twenty-first century, their heads may explode.

★ **And the Winner Is:** Keeping Baby Safe

Health officials in the 1950s urged parents to use wallpaper coated with DDT in their baby's nursery to get rid of flies that carried diseases.

One officially unanticipated side effect: the DDT wallpaper made more kids sick than the flies did.

THE DON'T CALL IN THE MORNING PRIZE:
FOR THINGS THEY DIDN'T TEACH
DOCTORS IN MEDICAL SCHOOL

★ **Third Place:** Eat a Fatal Diet

Sylvester Graham was a nineteenth-century health faddist who developed graham flour and the graham cracker to improve the American diet. But Graham's own diet became so restrictive that his health rapidly collapsed. He died at fifty-seven from trying too hard to be healthy.

★ **Runner-up:** Filter Filth

In the 1800s British military doctors advanced the notion that soldiers should grow mustaches to filter out battlefield infections and protect themselves from the filth of battlefield hospitals.

Doctors later found that soap and water used to clean up the filth worked even better than mustaches to protect against infection.

★ **And the Winner Is:** More Tea

In the 1700s when Dutch sailors brought tea back from China, the people of Holland fell for the new drink in a big way, as a health restorative. One Dutch doctor prescribed tea for his patients—two hundred cups a day.

THE FRIENDS OF PROZAC PRIZE:
FOR WINNING SOLUTIONS TO DEPRESSION

In 1931 President Herbert Hoover somehow missed the impact of the Great Depression when he offered this solution: "If someone could get off a good joke every ten days, I think our troubles would be over."

That was one of the few jokes heard during the economic nightmare, when one of every four working people was out of work. The Depression wasn't lifted until Hoover was kicked out of the White House by voters who had lost their sense of humor.

THE TRIPLICATE AWARD:
FOR RESEARCH INTO WHY WE DON'T WANT THE GOVERNMENT IN CHARGE OF OUR BUSINESS

★ **Third Place:** Quiet Beepers

Construction companies were faced with an interesting dilemma caused by conflicting government safety regulations.

One rule required the companies to outfit their heavy equipment with beepers so workers could tell when the machines were backing up. Another safety regulation insisted that companies outfit their workers with earplugs to protect their hearing from loud noises at the work site—noises like the beeping of equipment in reverse gear.

★ **Runner-up:** The Cure

Scurvy was the seafarers' scourge in the years after Columbus discovered the New World. On those long ocean voyages, crews were decimated by the disease, which caused debilitating body aches and prevented sores and wounds from healing.

Navies found their fighting forces laid low, not by enemy cannon, but by a disease whose simple cure was already known—but not to them.

For years some sailors reported that their scurvy was cured by eating citrus. Lemon trees were planted at the tip of South Africa so ship captains could reinvigorate their men on the long journey around the cape. The Atlantic island of Curaçao was named for the cure—citrus trees that grew on the island cured sailors of scurvy.

Yet the disease continued to ravage the navies and merchant fleets of Europe. In the early 1700s, an English doctor conducted experiments on sailors struck down by scurvy, which proved that lemon juice would cure them within days. Nothing else the doctor tried helped his patients.

Still nobody in a position to spread the word or change shipping regulations, or even give official advice, did anything about it.

It took another fifty years before the English government ordered that lemons and limes be included as a provision on all English ships going to sea. Much to their surprise—no more scurvy.

That's when English sailors came to be known as Limeys. Somehow English officials escaped being known as dunderheads.

★ And the Winner Is: The Dunderheads

In 1822 Norwegian traders made the first shipment of blocks of ice to England to meet the increased demand for ice among Britain's rising middle class.

But English customs officials refused to allow the ship to unload because they didn't know how to classify the ice for the purpose of import taxes.

By the time officials figured it out and ruled that ice was a form of dry goods, it wasn't. All the ice on the ship had melted into water. Have a nice trip back to Norway, fellas.

Great Moments in Dumb Predictions

1. Charles Duell, commissioner of the U.S. Office of Patents, in 1899—"Everything that can be invented has been invented."

2. Oxford professor Erasmus Wilson—"When the Paris Exhibition [of 1878] closes, electric light will close with it and no more will be heard of it."

3. The *Literary Digest* in 1899—"[The automobile] will never, of course, come into as common use as the bicycle."

4. A Western Union executive rejecting a new technology in 1876—"This 'telephone' has too many shortcomings to be seriously considered as a means of communication. The device is inherently of no value to us."

5. Lord Kelvin, president of England's Royal Society in 1895—"Heavier-than-air flying machines are impossible."

6. Sir John Ericksen, British surgeon to Queen Victoria in 1873—"The abdomen, the chest and the brain will forever be shut from the intrusion of the wise and humane surgeon."

7. Marechal Ferdinand Foch, professor of military strategy at France's École Supérieure de Guerre, in the days before World War I—"Airplanes are interesting toys, but of no military value."

8. President Lyndon Johnson—"It's going to be soon when nobody in this country is poor."

9. In 1956 comedian Jackie Gleason reassured a nation of worried parents that America would survive Elvis. "He can't last," Gleason said. "I tell you flatly, he can't last." And away you go, Jackie.

10. Samuel Pepys was one of the arbiters of British society in the early 1600s. As such, he declared a new play "the most insipid, ridiculous play I ever saw in my life."

What so upset him? Shakespeare's *A Midsummer Night's Dream.*

THE EVERYONE'S NOT A CRITIC AWARD:
FOR SHAMELESS SELF-PROMOTION

Eighteenth-century botanist Carl Linnaeus reviewed his own book *Systema Naturae* with this thoughtful assessment: "a masterpiece that can never be read and admired enough."

THE ALL-HOOSIER TROPHY

When Dan Quayle was a senator from Indiana, before he became vice president under George Bush the First, he defended his state from a rival politician who denigrated Hoosiers. The controversy caused people to ask once again, "Exactly what is a Hoosier?"

Quayle's answer was to introduce a Senate resolution to define a Hoosier as "someone who is smart, resourceful, skillful, a winner and brilliant."

Okay, but then what is a Tarheel?

THE 1,000 EDITORS AWARD:
FOR BEST USE OF EDITORIAL JUDGMENT

Where would writers be without editors? We'll never know because editors always have the last word, being closer to the press.

But imagine what it was like for writers in the centuries before the invention of the printing press, when all books were copied by hand. Many of the men who did the copying couldn't resist that editorial urge to tinker.

Take Chaucer's famous *Canterbury Tales*, if you could find it. The work does not exist in the Chaucerian original. We know it today only through the efforts of the copyists. Their edited variations differ from each other and whatever Chaucer wrote. The tinkerers had the lasting word.

THE BROTHERHOOD OF CENSORS PRESENTS THE ＿＿ AWARD: FOR BRILLIANT MOMENTS IN LITERARY REDEFINITION

★ **Third Place:** ＿＿＿ Theater

In the 1990s, to keep the community safe from the onslaught of the indecent, a high school in Chehalis, Washington, canceled performances of two shocking school plays: the musical *South Pacific* and Shakespeare's *A Midsummer Night's Dream*.

★ **Runner-up:** ＿＿＿ Satire.

Voltaire's satirical novel *Candide* ridiculed government authorities. In 1929 the book was declared obscene by U.S. Customs. At the time the book was banned, it was also assigned reading at Harvard University.

★ **And the Winner Is:** ＿＿＿ Fantasy

Lewis Carroll's *Alice in Wonderland* was banned in China in 1931 because in the story animals spoke human language.

Humans not getting the joke were declared perfectly legal by officials who didn't get it.

THE RECRUITMENT POSTER PRIZE

"That was one nice thing about the army," writer William McGivern pointed out, "someone else was paid to do the thinking."

THE EXPERT SPECIALIST PRIZE

Violinist Ruggiero Ricci wrapped it up by saying, "A specialist is someone who does everything else worse."

Chapter 4

Winning Mind Games:
All-Star Shockers, Psych-Outs,
and Gross Champs

The offensive, the rowdy, the people who make you wonder where they get the nerve—they try just a little bit harder to rise to the bottom. Shouldn't they be rewarded for their efforts? No, I suppose they shouldn't. But too late.

THE SHOCKERS ALL-STAR TEAM

ALL-STAR DEFENDERS

In 1966 Christian groups in the United States rose up to protest the music of a shocking rock 'n' roll band, burning their records, demanding that radio stations ban their music. The group? Those radical, heretical Liverpuddlians, the Beatles, who only wanted to hold your hand.

ALL-STAR TOPLESS

In 1935 on the beach at Atlantic City, police arrested swimmers for going into the ocean naked from the waist up. No, not women. They arrested men for swimming without shirts.

ALL-STAR BOTTOMLESS

Ever had that dream where you show up at school or work and everyone is staring at you? Suddenly, you realize—you're naked.

In 2003 two airline pilots turned that dream into their own daring reality when they flew their Southwest 737 naked.

"Ladies and gentleman, this is your captain speaking. If you will look out the left side of the aircraft, you will see some very surprised geese."

THE HEAVY BREATHER

Hermippus, an educator in ancient Rome, claimed to have found the secret to a long life: breathing in the expirations of young girls to absorb their purity.

THE EXPLODING DENTAL PATIENT

When celluloid was invented in the 1800s, it was used to produce false teeth. Celluloid choppers worked okay until dentists and their patients found one unfortunate side effect—every now and then the teeth exploded.

AWARD-WINNING
PUBLIC DISPLAYS OF OUTRAGE

THE LEWD NUDE PRUDE MEDAL: FOR SHOCKING ART

★ **Third Place:** *The Last Judgment*

In 1933 an art history textbook with photos of the Sistine Chapel and Michelangelo's painting of *The Last Judgment* was impounded by a U.S. Customs official for containing "lewd pictures."

★ **Runner-up:** *David*

Italian art lovers who attended the unveiling of Michelangelo's statue of David were shocked by the statue's nudity. They threw stones at what was later recognized as a masterpiece.

★ **And the Winner Is:** Venus

In Germany in 1853 a statue of Venus de Milo was arrested and tried for public nudity. The artist being unknown and dead for several centuries, the statue itself was convicted.

THE PICKY CRITIC PRIZE: FOR EXPANDING THE BOUNDARIES OF CRITICISM SO THAT JUST WHEN YOU THINK EVERYTHING HAS BEEN KNOCKED, THEY FIND SOMETHING ELSE TO SLAM

★ **Third Place:** The Vile Phrase

In the 1860s writer Nathaniel Hawthorne blasted a new development in the funeral industry: the casket. Prior to that time, people were buried in plain boxes, if boxes were used at all. Hawthorne called the newfangled, fancy casket "a vile modern phrase."

★ **Runner-up:** The Weak Hitter

Stan Musial was having a great game against pitcher Bobo Newsom, touching him for a single, triple, and homer. When Bobo was finally taken out for a reliever, he was asked if Stan the Man had any weaknesses.

"Sure," Newsom said, "he can't hit doubles."

★ And the Winner Is: The Bather

In the eighteenth century an English person who took a bath was considered eccentric. The English writer Samuel Pepys was surprised when he learned that his wife had taken a bath—once in her life. But he was shocked when she announced that she intended at some point to take another.

THE SEMI-SHOCKING PRIZE:
FOR FAMOUS PEOPLE WHO DID THINGS
YOU WOULDN'T THINK THEY'D DO

★ Third Place: The Opening Act

President Ronald Reagan played Vegas in 1954, long before he went into politics. His act? General clowning around and wrestling with the bandleader. Maybe that's how he got ready for D.C. politics.

★ Runner-up: The Bird Lover

An animal lover who shot animals? That would be the naturalist John Audubon. When he wasn't saving wild life, he was shooting hundreds of birds so he could pose them for his bird paintings.

★ And the Winner Is: He Did What?

Harry Truman, later to become our thirty-third president, joined the Ku Klux Klan in 1922 so he could get elected as a judge in Missouri. He quit the Klan when he found out they were bigots.

GREAT MOMENTS IN THE HISTORY OF SHOCK 'N' ROLL:

1. When Elvis first sang on national TV in 1955, the cameras showed his performance from the waist up only. Producers of *The Ed Sullivan Show* considered the Presley pivoting pelvis too suggestive for a sexually repressed society to handle.

2. In 1957 the Chicago archdiocese banned rock 'n' roll music from Catholic schools because "Its rhythms encourage young people to behave in a hedonistic manner."

3. In 1962 New York City's Catholic school students were instructed to stop dancing the Twist because Chubby Checker's monster hit was un-Christian. Some of them must have kept dancing because "The Twist" hit number one on the charts twice and stayed around the top of the charts for nine months.

4. Rocker P. J. Proby was dropped from the '60s TV show *Shindig* because he had developed a stage routine of splitting his pants during concerts. Producers were afraid he'd split on TV.

5. Numerous radio stations across the country banned "(I Can't Get No) Satisfaction" by the Rolling Stones in 1965 because of the song's suggestive lyrics.

6. Then in 1967 the Rolling Stones agreed to change a few of the words in their song "Let's Spend the Night Together" so they could appear on Ed Sullivan's show. The title line was changed temporarily to "Let's Spend Some Time Together."

7. During the halftime show of the 2004 Super Bowl, singer Justin Timberlake removed part of singer Janet Jackson's shirt to reveal one of her star breasts on national TV. This upset viewers who had tuned in to watch rapper Nelly grab his crotch.

Elvis could be heard laughing as he left the building.

The Gotcha Club presents the Psych-Out Awards for people who know that convincing you they're going to win makes winning a whole lot easier:

THE SIGMUND "KILLER" FREUD MEMORIAL PLAQUE:
FOR BEST USE OF THE PSYCH-OUT
TO ENHANCE ATHLETIC PERFORMANCE

★ **Third Place:** The Animal

Arm wrestler Bruce "the Animal" Wayne psyched himself up for championship matches by eating live crickets, washing them down with motor oil.

★ **Runner-up:** The Gentleman

British arm-wrestler champion "Gentleman" Les Clayden psyched his opponents by showing up for matches dressed in a suit and bowler hat.

★ **And the Winner Is:** The Undefeated

The greatest gladiator of all time, the Greek warrior Theogenes, was a champion in the sport of metal-spike, to-the-death boxing.

Theogenes won 1,425 consecutive bouts—killing all of his opponents. Don't you think that after the first 1,100 or so, the rest of the competition was a little psyched-out going into the ring?

THE NOTHING SELLS LIKE FREE PUBLICITY AWARD:
GOES TO ROCK 'N' ROLLERS EVERYWHERE

★ **Third Place:** Paul

In 1972 Paul McCartney's song "Give Ireland Back to the Irish" was banned from airplay by the BBC in England. The ban immediately turned the record into a hit, one of the rare times a political song climbed into the Top 20.

★ **Runner-up:** The Sex Pistols

In 1979 the Sex Pistols released their scathing version of "God Save the Queen" to coincide with Queen Elizabeth's Silver Jubilee. British radio immediately banned the song because of its "treasonous sentiments."

The record soared to number one on British charts.

★ **And the Winner Is:** The Rapping Salesmen

In 1990 the CD "As Nasty as They Wanna Be" earned 2 Live Crew the distinction of becoming the first rappers hauled into court on obscenity charges.

The charges were dropped, and the publicity racked up big sales.

Neatly done, all, and without having to pay for advertising.

THE BARGAIN BASEMENT TOP-SECRETS PRIZE

The Nixon administration tried to block publication of the Pentagon Papers in 1971 by classifying them government secrets. The papers indicated that the government had been misleading the American people about the Vietnam War for years.

When the courts ruled against the government efforts to keep the information secret, the papers were quickly published as a book. This created the incongruity of having information classified as secret by the Pentagon that was available in a book to anyone who went into the Pentagon store to buy one.

THE UNPSYCHED PRIZE: FOR PEOPLE WHO WERE TOTALLY PSYCHED-OUT BUT GOT OVER IT

Thor Heyerdahl, an unlikely Norwegian adventurer, became famous in 1947 when he crossed the Pacific Ocean on a balsa log raft (defying the experts who said he'd sink after a couple hours at sea).

The dangerous journey followed Heyerdahl's theory of prehistoric human migration, which he wrote about in *Kon-Tiki*, a book rejected by a dozen publishers before it became a best seller.

Heyerdahl was the least likely candidate to cross a pond much less an ocean. As a child, he almost drowned twice.

At the age of five, he jumped through a hole in the ice of a frozen lake. But he survived. Seven years later, he fell through the ice of another frozen lake—and survived.

These close escapes left Heyerdahl with a fear of drowning. But the third time proved the charm. At the age of twenty-two, he almost drowned again but managed to swim to safety out of a raging river. After that, it was bring on the ocean.

The Society for the Disgustingly Challenged presents the Gross-Out Ribbons, for stimulating the gag reflex. (TV show contestants are not eligible for this prize.)

FOR WRETCHED ACHIEVEMENTS IN THE FIELD OF THE PERFORMING ARTS

Performance artist Ron Athey reminded us why we should always support the arts—as long as they take place in Minnesota, unless we are Minnesotans—when he staged a show called *Four Scenes in a Harsh Life* in Minneapolis.

During the show, the artist used a knife to draw blood from another performer, then soaked paper towels in the blood and hung them over the audience—if any remained by that time.

FOR ROYALLY REPULSIVE RITUALS

In the twelfth century the Irish crowned their kings with a pageant that included boiling a horse in a large tub. Then the king bathed in the tub. Then the king and his subjects ate the horse. Then they drank the king's bathwater.

Thus were king and his people united. Champagne and appetizers as an alternative menu was considered too French.

FOR THE IRISH EVEN IF THEY'RE NOT KINGS

In his novel *The Ginger Man*, J. P. Donleavy wrote about a character with a kingly vision: "When I die I want to decompose in a barrel of porter and have it served in all the pubs in Dublin."

FOR ABOMINABLE CURES THAT WERE WORSE THAN THE DISEASE

★ **Third Place:** Skull Powder
During the Dark Ages, doctors treated the insane by dosing them with medicine made from the pulverized skulls of corpses. And we thought the cows were mad.

★ **Runner-up:** Fly Mash
In the 1800s you could buy a popular cure for baldness—a paste made of mashed flies. Didn't actually grow hair but at least it got rid of a few flies.

★ **And the Winner Is:** Leprosy Drip

In the Middle Ages doctors convinced sufferers they could be cured of leprosy if they stood under a gallows when a criminal was hung and let his blood drip down on them. And you thought your HMO was tough.

For Scientific Research to Produce the Milk-Shot-Out-of-the-Nose Effect in Generations of Third Graders

Eighteenth-century astronomers Frederick and Caroline Herschel were brother and sister. Since astronomy wasn't then the high-paying field it is today, the Herschels made their own telescopes. Because they didn't have much money, they crafted the scopes' mirrors using molds made of horse manure. No kidding. And they made the world's best telescopes that way.

Using one of their manure scopes, they discovered a planet that was twice as far away from the sun as the planet next in line, Saturn. Proving that scientists do have a sense of humor, the Herschels rewarded schoolkids with endless giggles by naming their discovery Uranus in honor of the Roman god who was the father of Saturn.

But Uranus wasn't their first choice. They wanted to name the planet George, in honor of the King of England, George III—a funny name for a planet, but not the laugh-getter Uranus proved to be.

For Gross Pie on the World Menu

The Japanese make a pie out of earthworms.

For Outstanding Fly Collections

Can you get people to spend the summer counting flies? Yes, you can. But it's going to cost you $50.

In 1912 the Canadian city of Toronto held a contest to see which kid could kill the most flies. The kids of the city spent the summer swatting and entered 3 million dead flies in the contest.

The winner was a girl who turned in two hundred pounds of dead flies. Her prize? Fifty dollars. Dead flies at that time were a bargain at 25 cents a pound.

For Revolting Use of Mayo in a Nonsandwich Production

In Mel Brooks's movie *High Anxiety*, a Hitchcock parody, he gets chased by a flock of birds who poop on his head as he runs away.

How exactly does Hollywood simulate bird poop? They mix chopped spinach and mayonnaise. Now you know, but may not be glad you do.

For Tasteless Artistic Vision

Painter Pablo Picasso felt that the urge to create would conquer any attempts to suppress it, that even if locked in prison he would still be an artist, "even if I had to paint my pictures with my wet tongue on the dusty floor of my cell," he said.

FOR TRAINING MAN'S WORST FRIEND

Vasco de Balboa discovered the Pacific Ocean in 1513. Actually, the ocean had been right there for centuries, as the Indians knew but were too polite to point out.

Balboa's expedition of discovery included his favorite dog, Leoncico, who was paid an officer's salary. What was the dog's job? To lead his master's pack of dogs in charge of killing and eating Indian captives.

SPECIAL AWARDS OF GROSS MERIT

THE CLEANLINESS IS NEXT TO GOD-AWFULNESS PRIZE: FOR LESSONS THEY NEVER TAUGHT AT HAMBURGER UNIVERSITY

In 2004 two workers at a North Carolina fast-food restaurant were found using the kitchen sink to take bubble baths after work.

The men were caught when they took photos of each other bathing in the dishwasher's sink and had the shots developed at a local photo shop.

At least they weren't working on their tans under the heat lamps.

THE WHALE WATCHERS' WATCH OUT! WHALES AWARD: GOES TO THE EXPLODING WHALE OF TAIWAN

In 2004 university scientists on the island of Taiwan were trucking a dead sperm whale to the lab to find out why it had washed up on the beach.

As they drove through town, the whale suddenly exploded from the pressure of stored-up gas. Pedestrians for blocks were showered with flying whale guts. Sue, sue sushi, good-bye.

Chapter 5

Missing It Entirely:
Prize Ironies and Great Last Laughs

To err is human. To err over and over again is upper management.

Homo sapiens are the only species that appreciates irony—or has reason to. While most animals don't have an ironic bone in their bodies, we produce endless winners of the Awards for People Who Miss It Entirely.

HOW IRONIC IS THAT PRIZE?
THE AWARD THAT CAN'T BE WON UNLESS IT
SHOULDN'T HAVE BEEN WON IN THE FIRST PLACE

★ **Third Place:** The Movie Star
Bruce Willis lost his job as a spokesperson for Seagram's whiskey when he was arrested for drunk driving.

★ **Runner-up:** The President

Ronald Reagan's book *Speaking My Mind* was ghosted by professional speechwriters, who were speaking the president's mind for him.

★ **And the Winner Is:** The Queen

The historic ocean liner the *Queen Mary* was named by a slip of the ego.

The head of the company that owned the new ship intended to call it the *Queen Victoria*. But he was not specific enough when he told England's King George V that he was going to name it for the "greatest of all English queens."

Before the businessman could clarify his intentions, the king remarked, "Oh, my wife will be pleased." George's wife? Queen Mary.

THE FOB PRIZE: FOR TURNING A GOOD THING INTO NOTHING, GOES TO THE $1.00 WATCH

In 1892 American watchmaker Robert Ingersoll cornered a new market—pocket watches for the common man. He manufactured a cheap pocket watch and sold it for $1.00. His slogan: "The watch that made the dollar famous."

Ingersoll's company stayed number one for twenty years. It was so successful that when the newfangled wristwatch came into fashion during World War I, Ingersoll ignored it. Why would people want to wear a watch on their arm, he reasoned, when they could carry one on a chain in their vest pocket?

While other companies went into the wristwatch business, Ingersoll stuck with his best seller, the pocket watch. His company went broke by 1922.

THE ONE MORE TIME AWARD:
FOR PEOPLE WHO WHEN THINGS GO BAD KEEP ON GOING UNTIL THEY MAKE IT MUCH, MUCH WORSE

★ **Third Place:** The Hedgehog Hunters

American farmers in the eighteenth century hunted down and killed hedgehogs, believing they stole milk from cows, which farmers felt was their job.

Hedgehogs got a bad rap. They were actually helping the farmers by feeding on pests. Without the hedgehogs to protect them, farmers faced a pest infestation.

★ **Runner-up:** The Rice Beginners

When Ireland's potato crop failed in 1846, thousands of people faced starvation. Charities provided them with rice to keep them alive. But the Irish had no experience preparing rice.

Irish women cooked it for hours until the rice formed a mush that made people ill. They then tried to eat the rice uncooked, which make them even sicker.

★ **And the Winner Is:** The Hollywood Director

Michael Cimino had a surprise hit when he directed *The Deer Hunter*. This early success fooled Cimino (as it's fooled other Hollywood geniuses) into thinking he had the Golden Touch.

In 1980 Cimino decided to make the epic western *Heaven's Gate*, spending an epic budget to do it. He dug himself a deep hole by shooting a million feet of film (ten times as much film as most movies require). When that didn't work, he kept going and shot another half million.

The epic result: a film that bombed at the box office, destroyed Cimino's reputation, and, along with it, the fortunes of United Artists movie studio.

There's a certain irony to just about everything that happens to us, which is why the Irony Foundries of America present nominees for the Irony Hall of Fame.

POP STAR WARRIORS

Fans collect guitar picks from their favorite rockers or costumes worn by the stars. This harmless pursuit is a civilized derivative of the ancient custom of consuming the body of dead warriors or kings to internalize their power and heroism.

HARD WORKERS

In the 1800s Idaho City built up around gold mines, which almost destroyed the city. Enthusiastic miners bored so many holes under the town that buildings collapsed.

THE PETARD HOISTER

The powerful rarely get hoisted on their own petard. Why should they? They own the petards, upon which they find reason to hoist everyone else. But every now and then some big shot gets caught.

In 1964 Howard Smith, chairman of the House Rules Committee, came up with a clever strategy to defeat the proposed Civil Rights Act.

He didn't want to appear prejudiced by opposing a bill that protected the rights of racial minorities. So he added a provision prohibiting discrimination on the basis of sex. He figured the male chauvinists in Congress would vote down any measure that gave women equal rights.

Smith got his comeuppance when women activists joined civil rights activists to force passage of the bill.

THE ARRESTING OFFICER

In 1896 a New York City police captain arrested the exotic dancer Little Egypt for dancing naked at a stag party. The captain also arrested the guy who threw the party (one of P.T. Barnum's grandsons) for conspiracy to commit indecent exposure.

After that, the police captain himself was arrested for invasion of privacy.

P.T., the big-top showman, would have been proud of the whole circus. Charges were dropped all around

THE AVENGING LOBSTER

A California fisherman drowned off the coast of Redondo Beach in 2004 when he got snared by a lobster trap rope and was yanked off his boat into the ocean.

At the time he died, the man was poaching lobsters in an area where lobstering was prohibited.

THE EXPLODING BAKER

Guns don't kill people; stoves kill people. That's what a Wisconsin woman found out when she defied the odds by pre-heating her oven.

Before the woman and her husband left on vacation in 2004, he decided to keep his guns and bullets safe from potential burglars by hiding them in the oven.

He made one critical mistake—he forgot to tell his wife what he'd done.

When they got home from vacation, she turned on the oven to preheat it for dinner. That's when the stove started shooting bullets at them. They ducked behind the refrigerator for cover, and no one was hurt. But no one ate dinner either.

THE BUBBLY ICEMEN

In the early 1900s, consumer demand for ice grew greater than the amount of ice suppliers could cut out of frozen winter ponds and ship to warmer climes.

Scientists developed the first machines for manufacturing ice, but customers weren't buying the new ice. They thought the air bubbles in a block of manufactured ice were a sign of impurity.

The manufacturers tried to educate the public that air bubbles were not bad for them and that pond ice also contained air bubbles. The public wouldn't buy it. So the icemakers developed methods of forcing out the bubbles, which raised the price of ice.

One further irony: the purity of pond ice was always questionable. The companies that cut ice from frozen ponds used horses to drag off the blocks of ice. Horses produce impurities worse than air bubbles, and you can imagine how hard it was to clean up after horses on a frozen pond.

SMIRKERS ANONYMOUS PRESENT THE LAST LAUGH AWARDS

BEST UNDERWATER SMIRKING

Squid can mix their ink with mucus, then shoot it off to form a fake squid. This pseudobody fools would-be predators who think they're getting dinner and end up with a mouthful of squid mucus.

Meanwhile, the real squid jets off, laughing in a way that only another squid could appreciate.

MOST TWELVE-FOR-ONE LAUGHS

In 1989 the Minnesota Vikings made a trade that shocked the football world—although you didn't have to be a fan to spot a bad idea of epic proportions. The Vikings packaged five players and seven draft picks and sent them all to the Dallas Cowboys. What did the Cowboys send back? A single running back, Herschel Walker.

Walker was one of the best. But picture a running back on one side of the field and twelve guys on the other side. Now guess who's going down?

The Vikings—up one running back, down a potential starting squad—went nowhere. The Cowboys used their draft picks to cop three Super Bowl titles.

BEST ASTROLOGICAL LAST LAUGH

Most scientists dismiss astrologers' claims that the stars can influence our lives. But studies show that a larger proportion of successful scientists are Virgos than any other sign.

MOST CONVENIENT GOVERNMENT LOGIC

The U.S. government wanted a canal cut cross the fifty miles of the Isthmus of Panama at the end of the nineteenth century to speed up shipping to the West Coast.

The United States bought the rights to the land at the isthmus from France, even though France didn't own the land.

When Colombia, which did own the land, objected, U.S. operatives staged a fake revolution, then called in the Marines and the Navy to protect the rights of revolutionaries who didn't exist to land the United States didn't own.

Ten years later we had our canal. About a hundred years later, we gave it back to Panama, despite the advice from Senator S. I. Hayakawa, who said we should hang on to it because "after all, we stole it fair and square." I'm pretty sure he was kidding.

BEST CUSTOMER SERVICE SMIRK

In the 1800s train travel was the fastest way to get around the United States. Conditions inside the trains were filthy. Passengers sat with their luggage on their laps for days because tobacco chewers spit all over the floors.

To feed the passengers over long train journeys, stations maintained filthy restaurants that insisted travelers pay up front. As the food was being served, conductors would blow the train whistle. The unfortunate passengers were forced to run for the train, leaving most of the food on their plates. This food was then reheated and resold to the next trainload coming around the bend.

LONGEST DELAYED LAST LAUGH

When Christopher Columbus landed on the Caribbean islands of the New World, natives honored him with two gifts: corn and tobacco, which he in turn introduced to the Old World.

Corn reshaped both worlds. Without corn, no burger stands, no packaging, no modern life because corn derivatives are used to manufacture thousands of products beside popcorn.

In exchange for the gift of life, the followers of Columbus gave the natives annihilation. Millions of them were wiped out by European diseases, weapons, and righteousness—the curious European belief that whatever they wanted God meant them to have.

That other Indian gift, tobacco, proved to be the revenge, killing more of the invaders than any attempts at military resistance.

One last laugh: Americans took life-giving corn and turned it into an instrument of death, the corncob pipe.

THE BITTER IRONY PRIZE: WHEN YOU CAN'T
TELL THE WINNERS FROM THE LOSERS

The Great Fire of London in 1666 burned most of the city to the ground. But don't think of it as losing a city. Think of it as pest control.

The fire also destroyed most of the city's rats, which were carrying the plague that had been killing every third person in London—until the fire stopped the spread of the disease.

Great Moments in the Ups and Downs of the Human Race

WORST OF TIMES

The fourteenth century in Europe. Famine, flood, the worst winter in centuries, major earthquakes, invading Tartars—and, oh yes, 20 million killed by the Black Death.

On the bright side: so many people died that there was great loot left over for the few who survived, making many poor people upwardly mobile.

BEST OF TIMES

The fourteenth century in North America. No Europeans spreading disease, death, and religion. The living was easy, with plenty of food wandering on the hoof, plenty of open land, few neighbors or enemies crowding in.

On the dark side: the living was so easy it made the people hospitable. So when the first Europeans showed up wanting to move in, the natives let them.

THE ALMOST PRIZE: FOR PEOPLE WHO COULD HAVE BECOME FAMOUS BUT BLEW IT

★ **Third Place:** The Other TV

The Scotsman John Baird had a great idea, but no money and not much luck either. He invented the first television system back in 1923, but went broke trying to develop it.

Baird's system was mechanical. Other engineers working on television used electronic systems, and theirs proved far superior to the mechanical TV, so Baird got nowhere.

★ **Runner-up:** Anyone Want a State?

The colony of South Carolina was established in 1629 when King Charles I granted the land to eight lords. These men were so plagued by pirates, rebellions, Indian wars, and mismanagement that they gave Carolina back.

★ **And the Winner Is:** That Delicious Wenberg

In the 1800s Delmonico's, the top restaurant in New York City, introduced many popular dishes to American cuisine. Its most famous new dish was Lobster Newburg, which wasn't called Lobster Newburg at all but Lobster Wenberg.

That's because the recipe was given to Delmonico's in the 1890s by one of its regulars, a customer named Ben Wenberg.

But Wenberg lost his shot at food immortality when he caused a major disturbance in the dining room one night and got eighty-sixed by the management—not only from the restaurant but from the dish itself.

The Great but Late Award

Much greatness is lost to the world simply because it's not recognized by the keepers at the gate. Then there are the people whose greatness is only recognized when it's too late to do them any good. This award provides belated recognition of that belatedness.

★ **Third Place:** Louis Braille

Blinded as a child, Braille learned to read by touching twigs shaped into letters. He invented a fingertip reading code for blind people in 1829, but the system was not adopted.

He died in obscurity. Two years after his death in 1852, the Braille system was adopted as a standard.

★ **Runner-up:** Franz Schubert

Although he was always a prolific composer, Franz Schubert's music was ignored during his lifetime. He lived in poverty and died that way. Schubert's genius wasn't recognized until after his death.

★ **And the Winner Is:** Charles Ives

The American composer had to become an insurance executive because his work didn't achieve public recognition until Ives was near death in 1954.

SPECIAL NONRECOGNITION OF IRONIC MERIT FOR CHARLES BABBAGE: AN INVENTOR WHO WAS SO FAR AHEAD OF HIS TIME THEY WOULD HAVE NEEDED A COMPUTER TO CALCULATE IT, ONLY THEY DIDN'T HAVE A COMPUTER IN HIS TIME BECAUSE HE COULDN'T QUITE INVENT IT

Nineteenth-century scientist Charles Babbage worked most of his life trying to build the world's first computer. He died in 1871 without finishing the project.

His ideas were ignored in his lifetime. Not until computers became technologically possible in the next century was Babbage recognized for his pioneering work and his genius. I know that feeling, don't you?

THE LASTING IMPRESSION PRIZE: FOR THE GARBAGE WE LEFT BEHIND

The dozen Apollo astronauts who walked on the moon left their footprints behind. Because there is no wind or rain on the moon to erase them, those footprints should last for millions of years.

The same is true for the stuff they left behind on the moon's surface: moon buggies, six American flags, golf balls, and a family photo.

THE SECOND TIME IS THE HARDEST PRIZE: FOR PEOPLE WHO LET SUCCESS GO TO THEIR HEADS

Some people have a great initial success, then flop miserably when they try to repeat it. Obviously, that includes just about every film director who makes Hollywood sequels.

Their major failing? They ignored this advice: if by some miracle you do succeed, have the common sense to quit while you're ahead—or at least not quite as far behind as you could be.

★ **Third Place:** The Scientists

Our engineers and scientists have created the marvels of our age—and the threats too. As writer Stephen Vizinczey pointed out, "The truth is that our race survived ignorance. It is our scientific genius that will do us in."

★ **Runner-up:** The Second Canal

Everyone told him he'd never make it. Others had tried. They all failed. But French builder Ferdinand de Lesseps undertook a monumental and dangerous project in the 1800s. He built the Suez Canal.

Actually, twenty-five thousand Egyptian laborers built it. But De Lesseps put together the design, the money, and the manpower to pull off this marvel of engineering.

Swelled by his success, De Lesseps then attempted to build a similar canal across the Isthmus of Panama—and flopped miserably. He went bankrupt trying to make it work.

★ **And the Winner Is:** The Second Career

King Gillette spent six years experimenting before he successfully invented the safety razor and made millions. Gillette then jumped track and devoted his energies and fortune to promoting a new world order, where everything would be run by engineers for the betterment of mankind.

He had one other big idea: to convince people to stop cooking in their own kitchens and eat together in peace and brotherhood in huge dining halls, kind of like a summer camp that never ends.

Obviously, Gillette did much better with razors then he did with perfecting a world run by engineers. If you think that one still has a chance, see you over at the communal dining hall.

Chapter 6

The Occasional Crime Stoppers
of America Awards

Cruel and unusual punishment, it's against the Constitution. Who are we kidding? All punishment is cruel. If they locked you up in a hotel suite with room service, cable TV, and a swimming pool, that wouldn't be punishment. It would be the Holiday Inn.

As for unusual punishment, we've been punishing people for so long it's pretty hard to find an unusual way to do it.

"First, we're going to put this bag of gumdrops on your foot, the five-hundred-pound bag. Then we'll dye your hair lime green, and the rest of you too. Also, you have to watch *Fear Factor* reruns for the next ten to twenty years."

Now that would be unusual punishment.

Meanwhile, dumb crooks remain eligible for the Occasional Crime Stoppers of America Awards because if it wasn't for the stupid crooks who would the cops catch?

THE MS. BIG AWARD:
GOES TO THE MILLION-DOLLAR COLLAR

A Georgia woman was arrested for fraud in 2004 when she tried to pay for merchandise at a Wal-Mart with fake money. The woman piled up $1,000 worth of goodies and handed the cashier a $1 million bill.

The United States Treasury does not print a $1 million bill. But in the interests of justice, we'd all like to have seen the Wal-Mart cashier making change.

THE SPRING BREAK IS NOT A CRIME PLACARD:
GOES TO DAYTONA BEACH, FLORIDA

The annual spring break revels bring Daytona Beach a fortune and leave a college-grade mess. In 2004 the city decided to hammer home a civic-minded message by nailing signs around town that implored visitors, "It's all about respect."

College kids had apparently been getting the wrong message for decades—that it was all about chug-a-lugging and passing out on the beach. Three hundred of the signs were stolen overnight—but respectfully.

THE WEDDING BELL BLUES PRIZE:
GOES TO THE CUT-RATE KILLER

In 2004 a Kansas City woman tried to hire a hit man to kill her husband because he had gotten her pregnant and dumped her.

Because hit men don't advertise in the yellow pages, the woman ended up making the offer to a detective posing as a hit man. Low on cash, she offered the hired gun a share of her husband's Social Security benefits, plus her wedding ring—an offer that gave new meaning to the wedding vow, "Till death do us part." Under the theory that even criminals get what they pay for, the woman was arrested.

THE MUSICAL MASTERMIND MEDAL:
GOES TO THE FM FELON

In 1995 a man took over control of a New Zealand radio station, claiming he had a bomb. What were his demands? He wanted the station to play his favorite song, "Rainbow Connection" by Kermit the Frog.

THE NONMUSICAL CRIMINAL MASTERMIND PRIZE

★ **Third Place:** The Surprised Hostage

Two young Ohio robbers had a clever idea in 2004 for tricking a grocery clerk into opening the store safe. One of them would pose as a customer, while the other held a gun to his head. The clerk would have to respond to the threat to a customer's life by opening the safe.

The scheme might have worked too if the robber holding the gun hadn't fired it by mistake, killing his partner.

★ **Runner-up:** The Surprised Burglar

A Mesa, Arizona, man was arrested in 2004 for burglarizing a store while the store's video cameras recorded him in the act of breaking and entering. The store was a security shop that sold video cameras and surveillance equipment to other stores so they could catch burglars.

Most thieves would have thought twice about breaking into a surveillance store, under the theory that they just might maybe have antitheft cameras. Not our prizewinner.

★ **And the Winner Is:** The Surprised Vacationer

A man from the Florida resort town of Tarpon Springs was arrested for fraud when he rented out his mobile home to snowbirds for the winter months of 2004.

The con man's first big mistake: he rented the same home for the same months nineteen times to different people. His second mistake: he stayed in the home so the police knew right where to find him when way too many people showed up to move in.

THEY'LL NEVER FIGURE THIS OUT PRIZE:
FOR CROOKS WHO THOUGHT THEY HAD THE COPS FOOLED

★ **Third Place:** Fill This Cup

An Ohio teenager on probation for another crime in 2003 knew he couldn't pass the required urine drug test, because marijuana was going to show up in the sample. So he substituted a urine sample from a cousin.

Only one problem: his cousin's urine tested positive for cocaine.

★ **Runner-up:** Fake Officer Needs Fake Backup

In 2003 an Ohio man got carried away with pretending to be a cop. The man liked to dress up as a policeman and pull people over for traffic violations. When he got an argument from one driver he stopped, the fake cop called in real cops for backup.

When the real cops arrived on the scene of the crime, they arrested the fake cop.

★ **And the Winner Is:** Just One Area Is Off-Limits

In 2003 Missouri police, searching for fugitives, asked a man if they could look in his house, thinking the criminals might be hiding there. The man said they could search everywhere in his house but the garage.

The police then got a warrant to search the man's garage and found evidence that he was running a methamphetamine lab there.

THE SURPRISE CRIME STOPPER AWARD:
FOR SIMPLE SOLUTIONS TO CRIME
THAT NO ONE EVER THOUGHT OF BEFORE

In 2003 a robber passed a stickup note to a teller at a Virginia bank. The teller read the note, told the robber, "I can't accept this," and gave it back. The robber left the bank.

THE BIG JOB: FOR CRIMES TOO BIG TO GET AWAY WITH

In 2004 a thief in Redmond, Washington, stole an eight-ton cherry picker from a construction yard. How was the thief caught? Someone who worked at the construction company saw the huge truck in the thief's front yard with a for-sale sign hanging on it.

MOST ROMANTIC THIEF PRIZE

In 2003 a Chicago man was arrested for stealing a diamond ring from a jewelry store. His MO? He asked the clerk to see the ring, then swallowed it.

The thief should have pled guilty to love, which the court might have interpreted as a form of insanity. He wanted the ring to give to his girlfriend when he proposed.

THE DISORGANIZED CRIME MEDALLION: GOES TO THE NONDENOMINATIONAL MAFIA, FOR BEST SENSE OF TIMING

New York Italian-Americans held a 1971 rally to protest the way they were stereotyped as mobsters. During the rally, mob boss Joseph Colombo was shot by a rival gangster.

THE CRIMINAL INJUSTICE PRIZE: GOES TO ENGLAND

Lord Mansfield, a chief justice of England in the eighteenth century, passed this sentence on a thief: "There is nothing wrong with you that a good hanging won't cure." That's probably true of most people.

STOP THE BEAT AWARD: FOR CONTINUING EFFORTS TO GET PEOPLE TO STOP DANCING

In the 1920s several states passed a law making it illegal for couples to dance for longer than eight hours straight.

You might think: Not much of a problem there. But a marathon dance contest craze had swept the nation. Couples danced until they dropped. Last man and woman moving to the beat were the winners. These contests literally dragged on for days, leading to serious injuries.

Great Moments in the Downward Advancement of the Human Race, There Oughta Be a Law, and There Is Division

State legislators often feel not enough people are getting thrown in jail, particularly the people who don't vote for them. So at various times, they passed laws making it illegal in these states to:

California: drive a car wearing a housecoat.

Washington: walk down a city street if you have a cold.

Oregon: use a can of corn as fishing bait.

Wyoming: take a photo of a rabbit without a permit.

Montana: open your spouse's mail.

Colorado: ride a horse while drunk.

Utah: fish while riding a horse.

Idaho: fish while riding a camel.

Nevada: ride a camel on an interstate highway.

New Mexico: vote if you're an idiot.

Arizona: let a mule sleep in your bathtub.

Missouri: own a bathtub with animal paw legs.

Kansas: catch a fish with your bare hands.

Nebraska: give a member of your family a perm without a license.

Iowa: kiss for more than five minutes.

Oklahoma: eat a hamburger that belongs to another person.

Indiana: walk down a road at night wearing your own taillights.

Wisconsin: kiss while riding a train.

Michigan: make love in a car unless the car is parked in your own driveway.

Minnesota: ride a motorcycle without a shirt.

Illinois: fish while riding a giraffe.

Ohio: give whiskey to fish.

Pennsylvania: sweep dirt under the rug in your house.

North Dakota: sleep with your shoes on.

South Dakota: sleep inside a cheese factory.

South Carolina: play a pinball machine if you're under eighteen.

North Carolina: plow a farm field with an elephant.

Texas: milk someone else's cow.

Alaska: wake up a bear to take its picture.

Hawaii: put coins in your ears.

Rhode Island: string a rope across a road.

Massachusetts: overeat at a wake.

Maine: keep Christmas decorations up on your house after January.

Connecticut: break the highway speed limit while riding a bike.

Vermont: whistle while swimming underwater.

New Hampshire: sell your clothes to pay gambling debts.

New York: walk down the street on Sunday with an ice-cream cone in your pocket.

New Jersey: slurp soup.

Delaware: get married on a dare.

Maryland: throw hay bales from second-story windows within city limits.

Georgia: curse at a corpse.

Florida: sing in public while wearing a bikini.

Kentucky: throw eggs at politicians during campaign speeches.

Mississippi: seduce a woman by lying to her.

Louisiana: make fun of a boxer during a boxing match.

Tennessee: carry a skunk across state lines.

West Virginia: hold elected office if you've previously taken part in a duel.

Virginia: hunt a raccoon after 2 A.M. on Sundays.

Arkansas: keep an alligator in your bathtub.

Alabama: wear a phony mustache if it makes people laugh in church.

STOP THE JOGGERS AWARD

In the seventeenth century, the Connecticut colony passed a law prohibiting running on Sunday. This was not an antijogging ordinance. Walking on Sunday was also against the law unless it was to or from church.

THOUGHTFUL LAWMAKERS AWARD

Dueling is illegal in Paraguay unless both fighters are blood donors.

THE PRISON PRIZE: FOR IRONIES YOU CAN PONDER WHILE SERVING TIME

★ **Third Place:** The Most Popular Prison

In 1992 Maryland built its new Baltimore County lockup to be state of the art and escape-proof. But there were a few bugs in the system.

Observation cameras burnt out. The computer controls that locked the cell-block doors wouldn't open them to let the guards out. Other locked doors burst open, which frequently defeated the whole concept of a prison as a place that kept prisoners in.

As for the shatterproof windows—as good as advertised. No one could break those windows. So nine inmates kicked the windows out of the window frames and escaped through the holes where the windows should have been.

★ **Runner-up:** Most Ironic Prison

In the fourth century, St. Quentin was freed from prison by an angel. He returned the favor after he was martyred by cutting the rope of a thief being hung.

The irony? America named one of its toughest prisons, San Quentin, in honor of a saint who freed the imprisoned.

★ **And the Winner Is:** The Best Answer to the Number-One Jailhouse Question—What Are You in For?

Felony exercise.

Fitness was once considered a dangerous political idea—in Germany of all places, in the 1800s.

A radical university student named Friedrich Jahn developed a system of gymnastics to get Germans into better shape so they could beat up those French bullies in the next war (which everyone knew would be coming as soon as they caught their breath from the last war).

Pudgy German officials didn't want to give up any power to fit young university students. So Jahn was arrested and his gymnasts persecuted for antiestablishment muscles.

THOSE RUSSIANS, WHAT A SENSE OF HUMOR AWARD

Russian writer Fyodor Dostoyevsky was arrested in 1849 for the crime of talking about a revolution. He was put in front of a firing squad . . . and then not shot.

Psych, Fyodor, it's only a fake execution. His ten-year exile to Siberia was not a fake.

THE CAR SALESMEN SUPPORT GROUP TROPHY:
GOES TO THE DEAL THAT WAS TOO GOOD TO PASS UP

Most teenage boys can't walk into a car dealership and drive out with a BMW. So our bright boy had the car delivered instead.

In 2004 a sixteen-year-old ordered a $123,000 BMW 760Li by phone. He told the dealer his bank would confirm a wire transfer.

Then the boy called the dealer and posed as a banker to confirm the transfer of funds. The dealer actually delivered the BMW to the boy at his high school.

Then the con boy got greedy. He tried to order a second car, and the dealer finally got suspicious. The boy was arrested. The first BMW was found in North Carolina, where he'd sold it.

THE THIEVES HI-IQ AWARD

No experience? No qualifications? No brains?

No problem. Crime is an equal-opportunity employer, open to anyone who expresses a sincere desire not to work for a living.

★ Third Place: Wrong Door

In 2002 a burglar broke into a Hollywood apartment, assuming it was empty. It wasn't.

When he heard people inside, the burglar ran out the door—only it was the wrong door. He ran into the closet instead. By the time he got out of that embarrassing position, found the front door, and ran downstairs, the police were there waiting for him.

★ Runner-up: Wrong Switch

In 2002 a man in Erie, Pennsylvania, couldn't understand why his electricity bill had skyrocketed. Neither could the power company. The man called the police. They found that a neighbor was stealing his electricity.

What kind of clever detective work did the cops do to figure this out? They followed a power line that trailed from the man's circuit breaker over the fence to the neighbor's house.

Why did the neighbor try such a dumb stunt? He needed the extra free power to reduce the cost of the lights he used to grow marijuana plants indoors. Double-busted!

★ **And the Winner Is:** Wrong Video

In 2002 Pennsylvania police recovered a stolen van. Inside, they found a receipt from a video store, where the thief had rented a video game prior to stealing the van.

What video game? *Grand Theft Auto 3.* On that receipt? The thief's name and home address, of course. Busted.

THE FAST-THINKING ANTICRIME PRIZE

In 1959 after two teenagers were fatally stabbed by another teen, officials in New York City took immediate action. Radio station WCBS banned Bobby Darin's hit song "Mack the Knife."

THE ORIGINAL DEFENSE AWARD

A Mexican woman, posing as a plastic surgeon, opened a clinic in Mexico in 2002 and performed breast implants on one hundred women. But she used the wrong kind of silicone. The patients came out of the operations with distorted breasts.

When the fake doctor was arrested, she offered an unusual defense at her trial—that she wasn't guilty because none of the women would have been beautiful even with better breasts.

Criminals everywhere should take note of the possibilities of this line of defense. A bank robber, for example, might argue that his theft was irrelevant because no one who kept money at the bank was going to get rich anyway. Politicians caught taking bribes could point out that if they hadn't taken that one, they'd only be forced to take another bribe.

Chapter 7

Only in Hollywood:
The Anti-Oscars

S.J. Perelman, who made a fortune writing movie scripts, described Hollywood this way: "A dreary industrial town controlled by hoodlums of enormous wealth." But hey, that's showbiz.

The Anti-Oscars honor the people who make Tinseltown what it is today—exactly what it was in S.J.'s time, only wealthier and covered with so much glitz you can't see the dreariness underneath.

BEST INTELLECTUAL ACHIEVEMENT IN FILM

Directors, producers, and studio execs were disqualified for this award because of insufficient ammunition. So the Anti-Oscar goes to movie audiences.

As director Billy Wilder pointed out, "An audience is never wrong. An individual member of it may be an imbecile, but a thousand imbeciles together in the dark, that is critical genius."

Also, remember the first rule of Hollywood: if you have a movie script with two ideas in it, what you really have is a hit and a sequel.

BEST WRITING IN A NONSCREENPLAY

Actress Alicia Silverstone had her biggest moment yet in the spotlight when she starred in the comic romp *Clueless*.

However, Silverstone had her Hollywood star moment when she tried to explain the film's significance: "I think that *Clueless* was very deep. I think it was deep in the way that it was very light. I think lightness has to come from a very deep place if it's true lightness."

BEST ACTRESS IN AN IMPOSSIBLE SUPPORTING ROLE

Jessie Landis, who played Cary Grant's mother in *North by Northwest*, was fifty-four at the time the film was made. Her son Grant was fifty-five.

BEST ACTOR IN AN IMPOSSIBLE SUPPORTING ROLE

A tie between Sean Connery and Sean Connery.

Connery played Harrison Ford's father in *Indiana Jones and the Last Crusade*. He also played Dustin Hoffman's father in *Family Business*.

Connery was, in reality, only twelve years older than Ford and only seven years older than Hoffman.

BEST SCREENPLAY BASED ON BOURBON

When mystery writer Raymond Chandler was hired to write the script for *The Blue Dahlia*, the studio needed a rush job because star Alan Ladd was about to be inducted into the army.

To get the script done in two weeks, Chandler devised an unusual work routine: he ate no food, drank bourbon constantly, and had a doctor give him daily glucose injections to keep up his stamina.

A twenty-four-hour rotation of studio secretaries typed the script as he dictated it, and the pages were rushed off to the studio by limousine so the director could keep shooting while Chandler solved the murder.

BEST USE OF NICKNAMES

In the Golden Era of Hollywood, studio execs competed in one of the more obscure aspects of film production—giving their new stars sexy nicknames they hoped would catch on with the public and increase the take at the box office. Can you match the starlet with her improbable moniker?

The Stars	**The Nicknames**
Lauren Bacall	The Brazilian Bombshell
Carmen Miranda	The Mexican Spitfire
Ann Sheridan	The Threat
Lizabeth Scott	The Oomph Girl
Barbara LaMarr	The Look
Lupe Velez	The Too-Beautiful Girl

The Answers:

Carmen Miranda: The Brazilian Bombshell

Lupe Velez: The Mexican Spitfire

Lizabeth Scott: The Threat

Ann Sheridan: The Oomph Girl

Lauren Bacall: The Look

Barbara LaMarr: The Too-Beautiful Girl

BEST CAREER NONMOVE

Barbra Streisand's mother grew angry with director Otto Preminger after he chose Jean Seberg over Barbra to star in the biopic *Saint Joan*.

"Look at Seberg's career" since making that film, Preminger shot back a couple of years later. "You should thank me for not picking Barbra."

BEST STAR VS. STAR

To settle star squabbles, posters for the movie *Outrageous Fortune* were reversed in different regions of America, so stars Bette Midler and Shelly Long shared separate but equal top billing.

BEST DIRECTOR, POSTPRODUCTION

Cecil B. DeMille designed an elaborate set for his 1923 version of *The Ten Commandments* along the sand dunes of Guadalupe, on the central coast of California.

When he was through making the film, DeMille decided it would be too much trouble to dismantle the set and truck it back to Hollywood. So he had the entire set buried under mountains of sand.

BEST DEATH SCENE

When matinee idol Rudolph Valentino died in 1926, more than a million women tried to crowd into his funeral.

BEST USE OF COWS

Cowboy star John Wayne liked his milk fresh. So he kept a cow on the terrace outside his penthouse apartment in West Hollywood.

BEST USE OF CADILLACS

Elvis Presley was so impressed by a waitress at the Formosa Café in Santa Monica that he didn't leave her a tip. He left her his Cadillac.

BEST USE OF THE COMMAND, "ACTION!"

When football star Howie Long retired from the NFL and turned to making movies, he knew he had to do his own stunts. A football player was tough enough for anything Hollywood could dish out.

In the movie *Firestorm*, Long had to run through a series of walls on fire. Before he filmed that scene Long asked costar Scott Glenn for advice. Glenn had worked with fire in the movie *Backdraft*.

Glenn's advice: "Don't trip."

"That's your advice," Long asked him. "Don't trip?"

"That's it," Glenn said.

Long did trip while shooting the scene. But his athletic training paid off—he was able to catch himself before he fell into the flames and kept running.

BEST TRAINER

Actress Katharine Hepburn learned to be tough growing up in a tough family. "If I spoke out of turn at the family table, I'd have a glass of milk poured on my head by my brother or was told to shut up by my dad," she recalled.

That family environment paid off after she reached Hollywood. "When [director George Cukor] would raise his voice, I'd never listen," Hepburn said. "I'm sure that's why we got on."

BEST GAG RESPONSE

When comedians Groucho, Harpo, and Chico wanted to test a gag before they put it into one of their Marx Brothers films, they performed it for their brother Zeppo, who always played the straight man. If Zeppo liked the gag, they threw it out.

BEST PERFORMANCE BY AN ANIMAL

When movie star Joan Bennett got ticked off at gossip columnist Hedda Hopper, she shipped off a live skunk to Hopper's house. But the newspaper columnist got the last laugh, announcing in her column that she'd named the skunk Joan.

BEST DUELING QUEENS

When she was signed to play Queen Mary in the film *Mary of Scotland*, Katharine Hepburn asked the director if she could also play the role of Queen Elizabeth.

Costar John Carradine said, "If you played both parts, how would you know which queen to upstage?"

Most Romantic Twist

When Hal Ashby directed Ruth Gordon in the offbeat comedy *Harold and Maude*, she didn't think she could play an older woman having an affair with a much younger man.

"I told her to pretend she was an older man," the director said. Gordon did and had no further problems with the role.

Most Un-European

Movie actress Joan Hackett smoked a pipe off screen. "Why do people stare?" she wondered. "If I were Marlene Dietrich smoking a cigar, I don't think they'd stare. Do you have to be European to be permitted an idiosyncrasy?"

Best Use of Gas

In 1840 when laughing gas first became popular, it wasn't used as an anesthetic during surgery. It was a stage act.

People would buy tickets for a Laughing Gas Exhibition, during which male volunteers came up on the stage and inhaled the gas. The audience was then entertained by the men acting goofy. Hey, that's showbiz.

GREAT MOMENTS IN ORDINARY HOLLYWOOD NAMES

What's in a name? If you want to become a movie star, you should choose from being a hard worker, a naturalist, a real man, or a good son. It worked for these Hollywood winners.

1. Hard Workers—Sigourney Weaver, Ava Gardner, Holly Hunter, James Mason, Minnie Driver, Danny Glover, Gary Cooper, James Dean, Elijah Cook.

2. Naturalists—Mel Brooks, Sally Field, W. C. Fields, Sharon Stone, Natalie Wood, James Woods, Billy Crystal, Stan Laurel.

3. Real Man—Paul Newman, John Goodman, Gary Oldman, Nicole Kidman, Ingrid Bergman, Ronald Colman, Morgan Freeman, Dustin Hoffman, Uma Thurman, Liv Ullmann.

4. Good Son—Jack Nicholson, Charles Bronson, Woody Harrelson, Liam Neeson, Edward G. Robinson, Samuel L. Jackson, Greer Garson, Glenda Jackson, Emma Thompson, James Mason.

HOLLYWOOD VANITY AWARDS:
FOR MOST FLAMBOYANT CELEBRITY PERKS

Vain? Don't be silly, darling.

★ **Third Place:** Jennifer Lopez

The movie star and singer brings her own sheets when she stays in hotels.

★ **Runner-up:** Jeanette MacDonald

When the movie star was sent on an African tour, she had her people bring along her own sheets and ship in bottled Montana water.

★ **And the Winner Is:** Rock 'n' Roller David Lee Roth

After a concert, the Van Halen lead man would sit in the door of the band's tour bus and have the road manager douse his feet in Perrier.

THE SMALL SCREEN AWARDS:
FOR BEST USE OF TV TO GET IT ALL WRONG

★ **Third Place:** The Dog

In a TV appearance on the *Steve Allen Show* early in his career, a young Elvis was humiliated when his manager agreed to have the singer croon his big hit "Hound Dog" to . . . a hound dog wearing a top hat.

★ **Runner-up:** The Teenager

Henry Winkler became one of the most popular teenage juvenile delinquents in television history as Arthur Fonzarelli on the comedy *Happy Days*. He was also one of the oldest teens on TV because the actor was actually twenty-eight when he played the Fonz.

★ **And the Winner Is:** The TV Diet

Everyone knows that being on TV makes you look heavier, which can cause even normal people to feel too fat.

As a teenager, comedienne Gilda Radner went on an extreme weight-loss program. Why?

"I saw myself on TV and couldn't stand it," she said. "I looked chubby. So I lost weight and now people say, 'You look awful.' My arms and everything. But now I look normal on TV."

THE PRE-OSCAR OSCAR

In Hollywood creativity is great as long as you can copy it from someone else. You might think if a movie's really good, it doesn't matter what you call it.

For example, you could name your film *You Gotta Come See this Movie, I Really Need the Money*. But resist the urge to honesty if you want to make it big in Hollywood.

Instead, if you want to win an Oscar for Best Picture, name your movie after the name of your main character.

The Academy of Motion Pictures has breathlessly handed out seventy-six Oscars for Best Picture since Hollywood began patting its own back in 1928. Of those, twenty-seven have gone to pictures named for their main character—everything from *The Great Ziegfeld* (1936) through *Kramer vs. Kramer* (1979) to *Dances with Wolves* (1990) and *Shakespeare in Love* (1998).

WE LOVE YOU, YOU'RE MARVELOUS, REALLY, AWARD: GOES TO TV GAME SHOWS

Where would TV games shows be without contestants? About the same place reality shows would be without people dying to humiliate themselves in front of millions of strangers.

But game show production crews often make fun of the contestants. For example, if a woman appearing on the show wears clothes the crew consider too provocative, they call the woman a hooker offstage while the hosts are smiling at her onstage.

THE HOLLYWOOD WEDDING AWARD: FOR MOVIE STARS CONSIDERATE ENOUGH TO DO EVERYONE ELSE A FAVOR BY MARRYING EACH OTHER

★ **Third Place:** The Above-Average Volcano

French actor Jean-Pierre Aumont described being married to movie star Maria Montez as like "living on the edge of a volcano. Except that she was much better-looking than the average volcano."

★ **Runner-up:** Winning One Vote at a Time

When they were both in Hollywood, Jane Wyman was married to Ronald Reagan. They divorced before he went into politics.

"Not many women can say they voted for their ex-husband," Wyman said later. "Even fewer would want to."

★ **And the Winner Is:** Where Do You Go from Here?

When Fernando Lamas proposed to Esther Williams, he offered to take her away "from all this."

"Away from all what?" she countered. "I'm a movie star."

THE HOLLYWOOD MADNESS AWARD:
FOR THE INDUSTRY THAT DRIVES YOU TO IT

★ **Third Place:** Marlon Brando

"The principal benefit acting has afforded me," Brando said, "is the money to pay for my psychoanalysis."

★ **Runner-up:** Jane Fonda

"You spend all your life," Fonda said, "trying to do something they put people in asylums for."

★ **And the Winner Is:** *Fame*.

Screenwriter Christopher Gore wrote *Fame*, the movie about talented students at the High School of Performing Arts in New York City. One student, Doris Finsecker (played by Maureen Teefy), realized what was holding her back from fame: "I know there's nothing wrong with me. That's what's wrong with me."

That's a problem many Hollywood newcomers have, but they usually get over it and never have that worry later in their careers.

THE VALENTINO'S BATHWATER MEMORIAL PRIZE:
FOR CELEBRITY MERCHANDISERS WHO CAN
SELL STUFF MOST PEOPLE COULDN'T GIVE AWAY

★ **Third Place:** The Stripping Fan

In 1961 when New York Yankees Roger Maris and Mickey Mantle were chasing Babe Ruth's home run record, a Texas stripper paid tribute to both sluggers by billing herself as Mickey Maris.

★ **Runner-up:** Fine Coonskin Corks

Actor Fess Parker, who played Davy Crockett on TV, opened a resort and a vineyard when he retired from showbiz. His winery's gift shop sold little coonskin caps that fit over the corks in wine bottles.

★ **And the Winner Is:** Fab Linen

In 1964 when the Beatles were on their sensationally popular invasion tour of the United States, a company bought the hotel sheets they slept in, cut them up into small squares and sold them to Beatle fans. Sold out too, which is better than most people can do with dirty linen.

THE "WHAT-IS-SHOWBIZ?" AWARD

★ **Third Place:** Sincerity

"That's what show business is," British TV comedian Benny Hill said, "sincere insincerity."

★ **Runner-up:** Blood

"Boxing is just show business with blood," British boxer Frank Bruno said.

★ **And the Winner Is:** Luck

"Show business is really 90 percent luck," actor Tommy Steele said, "and ten percent being able to handle it when it gets offered to you."

THE "WHAT-IS-HOLLYWOOD?" AWARD: FOR ATTEMPTS TO MAKE SENSE OF TINSELTOWN BY FINISHING THE PHRASE: "HOLLYWOOD IS . . .

★ **Third Place:** From Radio Comic Fred Allen

". . . a place where people from Iowa mistake each other for stars."

★ **Runner-up:** From Director John Huston

". . . a cage to catch our dreams."

★ **And the Winner Is:** From Movie Star Marilyn Monroe

". . . a place where they'll pay you a thousand dollars for a kiss and fifty cents for your soul. I know because I turned down the first offer often enough and held out for the fifty cents."

THE "WHAT-ELSE-IS-HOLLYWOOD?" AWARD:
FOR CONTINUING ATTEMPTS TO MAKE SENSE OF THE PLACE BY TRYING TO FINISH THE PHRASE: "HOLLYWOOD IS . . .

★ **Third Place:** From Writer Wilson Mizner

"a sewer with service from the Ritz Carlton."

★ **Runner-up:** Italian Filmmaker Michelangelo Antonioni

"like being nowhere and talking to nobody about nothing."

★ **And the Winner Is:** Radio Personality Fred Allen

"a great place if you're an orange."

THE "WHAT IS TV?" AWARD:
FOR ATTEMPTS TO MAKE SENSE OF THE TUBE BY FINISHING THE PHRASE: "TELEVISION IS . . .

★ **Third Place:** Writer Gore Vidal

"so desperately hungry for material that they're scraping the top of the barrel."

★ **Runner-up:** Poet T. S. Eliot

"a medium of entertainment which permits millions of people to listen to the same joke at the same time and yet remain lonesome."

★ **And the Winner Is:** TV Talk Show Host David Frost

"an invention that permits you to be entertained in your living room by people you wouldn't have in your home."

GREAT MOMENTS IN
MAKING MOVIES BY THE NUMBERS

1 Is a Lonely Number; 2 for the Road; 3 the Hard Way; 4 Weddings and a Funeral; 5 Corners; 6 of a Kind; 7 Brides for 7 Brothers; 8 Seconds; 8½; 9 to 5; 9½ Weeks; 10; 11 Harrowhouse; 12 Angry Men; 13 Women; 14 Hours; 15 Malden Lane; 16 Candles; Stalag 17; 18 Again!; Who Are the DeBolts and Where Did They Get 19 Kids?; 20 Mule Team; 21 Hours at Munich; Catch-22; 23 Paces to Baker Street; 24 Hours to Kill; The 25th Hour; 26 Bathrooms; The 27th Day; 28 Up; 29th Street; The 30-Foot Bride of Candy Rock; 32 Short Films About Glenn Gould; Naked Gun 33⅓; Miracle on 34th Street; 35 Up; 36 Hours; The 39 Steps; 40 Pounds of Trouble; 41 Going on 30; 42nd Street; 43: The Petty Story; Ms. .45; 47 Ronin; 48 HRS.; The 49th Man; Attack of the 50-Foot Woman; 52 Pick Up; Car 54, Where Are You?; 55 Days at Peking; Passenger 57; 60 Glorious Years; The Fighting 69th; 80 Steps to Jonah; 84 Charing Cross Road; 90 Degrees in the Shade; 92 in the Shade; 99 Women; 99 and 44/100% Dead; 100 Men and a Girl; Shack Out on 101; Across 110th Street; Turk 182; 200 Motels; Badge 373; 400 Blows; Fahrenheit 451; The 500-Pound Jerk; 633 Squadron; 711 Ocean Drive; 1,000 Clowns; 1,001 Arabian Nights; THX 1138; 1492: The Conquest of Paradise; 1776; 1900; 1918; 1941; Airport 1975; 1984; 1990: The Bronx Warriors; 2,000 Maniacs; 2001: A Space Odyssey; 2010; Safari 3000; The 5,000 Fingers of Dr. T.; Red Line 7000; Detroit 9000; 10,000 Bedrooms; 20,000 Years in Sing Sing; 40,000 Horsemen; 80,000 Suspects; 1,000,000 Years B.C.; 5,000,000 Years to Earth; 8,000,000 Ways to Die; 20,000,000 Miles to Earth.

Chapter 8

The World's Greatest Lovers and Other Winners in the Battle of the Sexes

Psychologists tell us that loneliness is a major cause of depression among singles. As any single can tell you, it's the other singles out there who are the major cause of depression.

Finding someone special who shares a common interest is tricky when your only interest is how you can get away from all those jerks who think you share their only interest—themselves.

No matter how confusing it gets, women will be women and men will be men—at least if the Republicans have anything to say about it.

Meanwhile, men and women will be able to share two things: service ribbons from the Battle of the Sexes and maybe a shot at the World's Greatest Lovers Olympics.

SERVICE RIBBONS FROM
THE BATTLE OF THE SEXES

THE DISTINGUISHED SERVICE
CROSS FOR HEAVY LIFTING

The romantic custom of carrying the bride over the threshold began in ancient times, but it wasn't an act of love on the part of a smitten groom.

It was an act of self-defense. The groom carried the bride inside to make sure she didn't lose her virginity to the lusty gods of the earth.

THE SO-SO HOUSEKEEPING RIBBONS

★ **Third Place:** Comic Rhonda Hansome

"A man's got to do what a man's got to do," Hansome said. "A woman must do what he can't."

★ **Runner-up:** Newspaper Columnist Erma Bombeck

"My second favorite household chore is ironing," Bombeck confessed. "My first being hitting my head on the top bunk bed until I faint."

★ **And the Winner Is:** Hollywood Celebrity Zsa Zsa Gabor

"I am a marvelous housekeeper," the oft-married Zsa Zsa said. "Every time I leave a man, I keep his house."

PURPLE HEARTS

★ **Third Place:** Wounded by Explanations

At the University of Pennsylvania in 1993 a Jewish student opened his dorm window and shouted at some passing black women students, "Shut up, you water buffalo."

The male student was accused of racial insults. He claimed he wasn't being a racist, he was translating into English the Hebrew word *behemah*, calling the women fools and that fools could be found among every ethnic group—male college students, for example.

★ **Runner-up:** Double-Duty Wounds

Politician Joseph Choate praised the Pilgrim Fathers for the hardships they endured during the settlement of the New World.

"But let us give thought to the Pilgrim Mothers," he added in his speech. "For they not only had to endure everything the Pilgrim Fathers endured, but they had to endure also the Pilgrim Fathers."

★ **And the Winner Is:** Wounded Panties

During a 2003 game, a Brazilian soccer referee reached into the pocket of his shorts for a red card to call a foul on an errant player and pulled out a pair of red lace panties instead.

The panties didn't belong to his wife. The letter the ref received from a divorce lawyer however—that did come from his wife.

THE ARMY OF OCCUPATION MEDAL:
FOR UNUSUAL DISCOVERIES ABOUT MARRIAGE

★ **Third Place:** The Naked Vision

In Germany young women were promised a vision if they took off all their clothes on St. Andrew's Eve (November 29). Once naked, they would see the man they were to marry. And perhaps he would see them.

★ **Runner-up:** Husbands by Fire

In the Polish version of the celebration of St. Andrew's Eve, a young woman could envision her husband-to-be if she held a black cat over a fire. The cat was unlikely to have any further visions.

★ **And the Winner Is:** Sinless Sex

In the 1700s St. Alphonsus wrote a handbook for confessors, which explained that marital sex was not a sin as long as neither husband nor wife enjoyed it.

WAR OF WORDS COMBAT ACTION RIBBON

Actress Cornelia Otis Skinner starred in George Bernard Shaw's play *Candida*. After opening night, he sent her a telegram: "Excellent, greatest."

She wrote back, "Undeserving such praise."

He responded, "I meant the play."

But she got the last word in cables, "So did I."

THE HE SAID, SHE SAID AWARDS: FOR HOLLYWOOD
MEN AND WOMEN WHO TOOK ON EACH OTHER

★ **Third Place:** W. C. Fields

The comic actor slammed his costar, the voluptuous Mae West, by calling her "a plumber's idea of Cleopatra."

★ **Runner-up:** Carol Channing

The film and Broadway star commiserated with Grace Kelly, who gave up Hollywood to marry the prince of Monaco, and with British Princess Diana, who gave up. "Every girl is waiting for her prince to come," Channing said. "But why do they always have to look like Prince Rainier or Prince Charles?"

★ **And the Winner Is:** Tony Curtis

When his days as a matinee idol had long passed, the actor said, "I wouldn't be caught dead married to a woman old enough to be my wife."

THE HAZARDOUS DUTY MEDAL FOR BUNDLING

Teenagers may not believe this, but colonial parents often insisted that young men and women who weren't married share the same bed at night. Colonial houses were too small to have enough beds to go around.

The couples bundled into bedclothes that were knotted tight at neck, waist, and feet. But only they knew what went on under the covers. This practice lasted in the tiny colonial houses of Cape Cod until 1845.

GREAT MOMENTS IN THE
BATTLE OF WITS BETWEEN THE SEXES

FROM THE WOMEN

1. Writer Sue Grafton—"If high heels were so wonderful, men would still be wearing them."

2. *Ms.* magazine publisher Gloria Steinem—"I have yet to hear a man ask for advice on how to combine marriage and a career."

3. Comic Elayne Boosler—"When women are depressed they either eat or go shopping. Men invade another country."

FROM THE MEN

1. Writer Ambrose Bierce—"You are not permitted to kill a woman who has wronged you. But nothing forbids you to reflect that she is growing older every minute. You are avenged 1,440 times a day."

2. Cartoonist and theme park mogul Walt Disney—"I love Mickey Mouse more than any woman I've ever known."

3. Vertically challenged movie star Mickey Rooney—"A lot of people ask me how short I am. Since my last divorce, I think I'm about $100,000 short."

THE WORLD'S GREATEST LOVERS OLYMPICS

GOLD MEDAL IN THE SPRINTS

The bird called the swift hardly ever touches land. Swifts fly all the time—even when they are mating.

Their sex act starts high in the sky. Locked together like sky-divers, the two swifts plunge rapidly toward the ground for hundreds of feet before pulling out of the dive.

GOLD MEDAL IN THE MARATHON

Millipedes are leggy crawlers that have trumped Viagra without a doctor's prescription.

When millipede males get old and lose their sexual potency, they can suddenly become young again, developing new sexual prowess so they can go on procreating.

Guys, while you're turning green with envy and wondering how bad a millipede diet might taste (bad, very bad), consider this: millipede coitus has been known to last for hours.

GOLD MEDAL IN THE DECATHLON

German writer Gerhart Hauptmann once suggested to the enchantress of Vienna, Alma Mahler Werfel, that they must become lovers in their next lives.

Hauptmann's wife put him straight right away, saying, "Darling, I am sure Alma will be booked up there too."

Gold Medal in Gymnastics

Sea slugs are bisexual in a way you probably haven't encountered before, unless you live in San Francisco.

The slugs often have both female and male sex organs. Two sea slugs having sex take turns being the woman and the man.

By law in some states, a single sea slug could marry itself.

Gold Medal in Swinging

The clown fish (yes, like little Nemo) can change sex without going to the doctor. If a female clown fish dies, a male clown fish will switch and become a female, then find a male who may have been his buddy but now becomes his mate.

Gold Medal in Wrestling

Spiders in bondage? The male crab spider prefers a big woman, which is lucky because the female crab spider is ten times as large as her mate.

He tames her with plenty of foreplay. While caressing her, he uses spider webbing to tie her down to a leaf before daring to have sex with her.

WINNERS OF THE LOVERS' POPULARITY CONTEST

Most Popular

During one of the happier Roman eras, annual lotteries were held for unmarried women and men. The men drew the name of a woman from a box, and they became a couple for a year, after which their names went back into the drawing for next year's couples. Built one of the world's great empires, didn't they?

MOST LIKELY TO END UP IN EXILE

Napoleon Bonaparte, the French military genius who conquered most of Europe but not his own mouth, said, "Nature intended women to be our slaves. They belong to us, just as a tree that bears fruit belongs to a gardener. Women are nothing but machines for producing children."

MOST LIKELY TO BE SURPRISED TO LEARN THAT WEARING A SWIMSUIT IS NOT ACTUALLY AN OLYMPIC EVENT

In 2004 a sixth grade boy in Ohio was suspended for bringing to school the *Sports Illustrated* annual swimsuit issue devoted to the little understood sport of competitive bikini posing.

The principal sent him home for violating the school policy on lewd material.

The boy's mother defended her son, saying, "To me, it's American culture. He should not have taken it to school, but I don't think it's morally wrong for a child that's almost thirteen to look at it."

MOST LIKELY TO GIVE UP STUDYING INSECTS

The Kinsey reports by Alfred Kinsey became hugely popular in the 1950s as the first scientific study of human sexuality in behavioral detail. But Kinsey was not a sexologist. He was actually a biology professor specializing in wasp behavior when he was offered the opportunity to switch gears.

Most Popular Ex

According to Mia Farrow's biography, ex-husband Frank Sinatra offered to have Woody Allen's legs broken when Allen had an affair with Mia's adopted daughter.

Most Likely to Succeed Only with Groupies

Everyone knows that guys go into rock 'n' roll for the groupies. But guys in other fields also put down the women they love, kind of.

★ **Third Place:** Wrestlers
Professional wrestlers call their women fans arena rats.

★ **Runner-up:** Truckers
Long-distance truckers refer to professionals who sell their services at truck stops as lot lizards. If a passing car contains a pretty woman they can ogle, they call her a seat cover.

★ **And the Winners Are:** The Swordsmen
The guys from the Society for Creative Anachronism, who like to run around the park waving big swords, call a woman who would be unattractive in the Middle or other ages, a fubba-wubba, which means a fat ugly broad with a bad attitude.

Most Likely to Succeed Only with Frenchmen

French filmmaker Marguerite Duras maintained a typically French ambivalence toward men. "You have to be very fond of men to love them," she said. "Otherwise, they're simply unbearable."

MOST LIKELY TO SUCCEED ONLY WITH RICH MEN

British journalist Julie Burchill observed, "Wherever there are rich men trying not to feel old, there will be young girls trying not to feel poor."

MOST LIKELY ALWAYS TO COME IN SECOND IN THE BATTLE OF THE SEXES

In 1991 research by University of Pennsylvania scientists indicated that men's brains deteriorate faster than women's brains.

MOST LIKELY NOT TO GET MARRIED A SECOND TIME

Anyone who got married a first time.

Percentage of American men who say they would marry the same woman if they had it to do all over again: eighty.

Percentage of American women who say they'd marry the same man: fifty.

Apparently, 30 percent of the men aren't getting the message.

MOST POPULAR AT HOME

Denis Thatcher was married to the prime minister of England Margaret Thatcher. When a reporter asked him who wore the pants in his family, Denis replied, "I do. I also wash and iron them."

MOST POPULAR WITH PEOPLE WHO HAVE JUST BEEN KICKED OUT OF THE HOME

Writer Ambrose Bierce defined the confusions of marriage as "a community consisting of a master, a mistress and two slaves, making in all, two."

SEXIEST AND OVERSEXIEST

Advice columnist Ann Landers, who handled thousands of advice-seeking letters during her newspaper career, observed that "women complain about sex more often than men. Their gripes fall into two major categories: 1) not enough; 2) too much."

MOST AUTOMATED HOUSEKEEPER

Writer Beverly Jones pointed out: "Now, as always, the most automated appliance in a household is the mother."

MOST LIKELY TO REMAIN A BACHELOR BY POPULAR DEMAND

"Rich bachelors should be heavily taxed," English writer Oscar Wilde pointed out. "It is not fair that some men should be happier than others."

MOST LIKELY NOT TO RECEIVE ANY PROPOSALS OF MARRIAGE

★ **Third Place:** American Writer H. L. Mencken
"The only really happy folk," he said, "are married women and single men."

★ **Runner-up:** British Writer Saki
"A woman who takes her husband about with her everywhere is like a cat that goes on playing with a mouse long after she's killed it," he said.

★ **And the Winner Is:** British Writer J. B. Priestley
"Marriage is like paying an endless visit in your worst clothes," he observed.

MOST LIKELY NOT TO RECEIVE
DECLARATIONS OF UNDYING LOVE

★ **Third Place:** Irish Writer George Bernard Shaw

"When two people are under the influence of the most violent, most insane, most delusive and most transient of passions," he said, "they are required to swear that they will remain in that excited, abnormal and exhausting condition until death do them part."

★ **Runner-up:** British Writer Quentin Crisp

"Any partnership demands that we give and give and give," he said. "And at the last, as we flop into our graves exhausted, we are told that we didn't give enough."

★ **And the Winner Is:** American Writer Fran Lebowitz

"The second you meet someone you're going to fall in love with, you deliberately become a moron," she said. "It would be impossible to fall in love with any human being if you actually saw them for what they are."

Chapter 9

On the Job:
Slave of the Year Awards

Sunday afternoon sinks low when it's raining or you're stuck with someone you can't get away from, or both. But no matter how bad you feel on Sunday, going to work Monday morning is worse.

The great myth of our time is that we're significantly different than the slaves who built the pyramids.

There will always be people with monumental vision, and they'll always need heavy lifters to get the dirty work done. Guess who that is? Whether they use the lash or the 401(k), the years of drudgery don't change that much.

Except for one thing: in ancient times they didn't hand out Slave of the Year Awards. But we do, for on-the-job performance that stretches the boundaries of stupidity in the workplace.

Winners of the World's Worst Job Contest

Got a job that's going nowhere? It's not going nowhere as fast as these lousy jobs.

★ **Third Place:** Mad Servant

In eighteenth-century England, aristocrats judged insane were sent to an asylum that catered to the wealthy. Their servants had to go along with them. The servants, mad or just a tad peeved, were locked up along with their bosses.

★ **Runner-up:** Leech Gatherer

In the 1800s doctors used leeches to de-blood patients with a variety of ailments (and with more ailments to come after being overdrained of a precious bodily fluid).

To gather medicinal leeches, French and German workers walked through ponds hoping the leeches would latch onto their legs. A top-notch leecher could gather two thousand leeches a day that way.

★ **And the Winner Is:** Flea Trapper

In ancient Egypt, palace rooms came furnished with flea servants. Their job? To coat themselves with the milk of an ass and stand in the corner.

Why? To serve as a human flea trap, keeping the little nippers off the better class of people.

The Fed-up Teacher Trophy

As any teacher knows, those the gods wish to punish they assign to seventh grade. And if you're really in bad with the powers that be, you get to monitor the detention class.

One seventh grade teacher in a Missouri middle school finally cracked in 2004. When a fourteen-year-old boy serving detention kept acting out, the teacher duct-taped the boy to his desk.

Yes, the teacher was forced to resign. Was it worth the penalty to become a legend to middle school teachers everywhere?

THE PLUMBING PRIZE: BECAUSE BATHROOMS CAN BE FOR SO MUCH MORE THAN JUST . . . YOU KNOW

★ Third Place: The Warm-up Act

Before the French artist Henri Matisse began a day of painting, he locked himself in the bathroom and played his violin for two hours.

★ Runner-up: The Rehearsal

Newsman Eric Severeid set a high standard for intelligent commentary when he was a regular on the CBS Evenings News in the seventies. To rehearse his commentaries before he went on the air, he recited them to any person he met in the D.C. bureau while standing at the urinal.

★ And the Winner Is: The White House

President Lyndon Johnson once held a meeting and dictated a memo to his secretary while in the bathroom receiving an enema.

THE SECOND CAREER CUP: FOR FAMOUS PEOPLE WHO FACED THE QUESTION WHAT DO YOU DO AFTER THE THRILL IS GONE? AT LEAST ONE OF THEM CAME UP WITH THE OBVIOUS ANSWER—SHOES.

★ Third Place: The Poet on the Battlefield

During the Civil War, poet Walt Whitman served as a nurse, helping young Union soldiers by writing letters home for them.

In attics throughout the North are family heirloom letters written by one of America's greatest poets, whether the families know it or not.

★ **Runner-up:** The James Gang Gets to Work

The James Brothers were infamous bandits, feared and admired in the Old West because they were bold, daring, and quick with a gun. After Jesse James was shot in the back by an assassin, his brother Frank turned to a new occupation—he became a shoe salesman.

★ **And the Winner Is:** The Player

After he retired from the NBA, basketball star Charles Barkley demonstrated his clear thinking on the job front. When asked what he was going to do next, Sir Charles said, "I think work is one of the most overrated things in the world." A basketball star should know.

THE APPRENTICE PRIZE: GIVEN TO FAMOUS PEOPLE FOR UNUSUAL ON-THE-JOB TRAINING

★ **Third Place:** The Minstrel Brakeman.

Jimmie Rodgers, the Singing Brakeman, who became the father of country music in the 1920s, worked on the rail lines. Before he hit it big with his soulful country songs, Rodgers also sang with a minstrel troupe in blackface and with a Hawaiian band.

★ **Runner-up:** The Smashing Writer

After playwright-to-be Eugene O'Neill dropped out of Princeton University, he traveled to Argentina where he worked for the Singer Company, dismantling old sewing machines by whacking them with a sledgehammer.

★ **And the Winner Is:** The Cinematic Communist

In a 1914 spy movie *My Official Wife*, a young Leon Trotsky was cast in a small role. The experience convinced him to return to Russia and become a leader of the Bolshevik revolution.

Who knows how history would have changed if he'd gotten better reviews and a hotter agent.

ODD JOBS PRIZE: FOR FAMOUS PEOPLE WHO DID WORK YOU WOULDN'T THINK THEY'D DO

★ **Third Place:** The Nude Model

Before he became a movie star, Charlton Heston worked as a nude model for the Art Students League of New York City. He earned $1.25 per hour.

★ **Runner-up:** The Romantic Sewer Worker

After he became a movie star, Robert Redford served as sewer commissioner in Provo Canyon, Utah.

★ **And the Winner Is:** The Revolutionary Pastry Chef

Ho Chi Minh led the North Vietnamese in successful wars against the French and then the Americans. But before he became a revolutionary military leader, Ho Chi Minh was an assistant pastry chef at the Carlton Hotel in London, studying under the master French chef Escoffier.

OOPS TROPHY: FOR SCREWUPS THAT PAID OFF

★ **Third Place:** The Bankrupt Cartoonist

When Walt Disney began his career as a cartoonist (not in Hollywood but in Kansas City), he went bankrupt.

Disney started the turnaround by creating cartoons that were used not in movie theaters but as fillers in vaudeville theaters, to stall for time by diverting the audience while the next act set up.

After that, he did better—creating an entire industry for animated films, not to mention the whole theme-park thing.

★ **Runner-up:** Crumbling Real Estate

That famous hillside Hollywood sign started out in 1923 as Hollywoodland, a kind of billboard for a housing development.

But when the sign began to fall apart from neglect in the 1940s, civic leaders stepped in. They got the bright idea of removing the last syllable, fixing up the rest, and using it to advertise the movie industry.

★ **And the Winner Is:** The Failed Cure

When English scientist Joseph Priestley invented fizzy soda water in the eighteenth century, he wasn't thinking about a drink that might refresh. He thought soda water would cure one of the plagues of his era—yellow fever. It didn't. But it did make possible Coke, Pepsi, and all the rest of the sodas that have spread across the world.

ODD JOB TEST PRIZE: FOR JOBS THAT ARE HARDER TO GET THAN THEY ARE TO DO

★ **Third Place:** Can You Pass the Waist Test?

French Queen Isabeau was even more obsessed with thinness than your average teenage girl. The queen decreed that if a woman wanted a position in her court she must have a waist no larger than thirteen inches.

Several of her lady-in-waiting applicants didn't make the cut, but they died trying.

★ **Runner-up:** Do You Have What It Takes to Work at Hooters?

As waitresses know, men come to Hooters restaurants because you just can't beat those burgers. Ogling the help in their tight-fitting uniforms is just something men have to put up with to get some really good curly fries.

Still applicants for the job claimed to be shocked in 2004 when police found out that the manager at a Hooters in Southern California was secretly video taping the women as they undressed to try on their uniforms.

Trying on uniforms turned out to be a major part of the job test. The manager managed to make some two hundred tapes before he was busted.

★ **And the Winner Is:** Are You Over 65?

Most people are forced to retire by age sixty-five. But you'd have to be in your sixties before you'd would qualify for one job— becoming pope of the Catholic Church.

ODD WORK HABITS OF ODD WRITERS AWARD

★ **Third Place:** The Hard Worker

A Broadway play, in manuscript form, usually runs 120 to 140 pages, about a page for each minute of stage time. When Arthur Miller wrote a play like *The Crucible*, his first drafts would run to 1,200 pages. Just another writer who found out that writing is editing.

★ **Runner-up:** The Perfect Job

President Theodore Roosevelt was so taken with the early poems of Edwin Arlington Robinson that he gave the poet a job in the Customs House, requiring the writer only to show up, which Robinson did for four years while working on his poetry at the government's expense.

But when the next president, William Taft, came into power and demanded that the poet actually work for his salary, Robinson immediately resigned.

★ **And the Winner Is:** The Scrap Man

John Keats, the great romantic poet, wrote his poems on scraps of paper, which he hid between the pages of books or dropped around the house.

If it wasn't for the efforts of his friend Charles Brown to recover and reassemble these scraps, much of Keats's poetry would have been lost to the world.

THE CAREER ADVICE TROPHY

★ **Third Place:** How to Handle Job Offers

Singer Rod Stewart asked Elton John if he should accept an offer to sing "Pinball Wizard" for the Who's rock opera *Tommy*. Elton told him no way, "Don't touch it with a barge pole."

A year later, the Who asked Elton John to sing the same song. Elton grabbed his barge pole and took the offer. "I don't think Rod's quite forgiven me for that," he commented years later.

★ **Runner-up:** How to Succeed in Politics

What does it take to be a successful politician? A vast fortune helps. Moral values and principles? Not so important.

"People with high ideals don't necessarily make good politicians," Japanese politician Michio Watanabe said. "If clean politics is so important, we should leave the job to scientists and the clergy."

★ **And the Winner Is:** How to Break into Showbiz

Before he became a Broadway playwright George S. Kaufman worked as the theater editor at the *New York Times*. The producer of a failing play asked Kaufman how he could get the play's leading lady into the paper.

"Shoot her," Kaufman replied.

THE CORPORATE SURPRISE AWARD: GOES TO FOOTBALL

"Football combines the two worst things about America," the newspaper columnist George Will observed. "It is violence punctuated by committee meetings."

THE RETIREMENT TROPHY: FOR PEOPLE WHO
SAW THE LIGHT AT THE END OF THE WORK TUNNEL

When opera singer Lotte Lehmann retired, a younger singer commiserated that it must be terrible to realize you've lost your voice.

"No," Lehmann corrected, "what would be awful is if I didn't realize it."

THE DREAM JOB MEDAL

The ultimate dream job would be dreaming, wouldn't it? Next to that, playwright Jean Kerr observed that one profession would be overcrowded should a position ever open up.

"Even though a number of people have tried," she wrote, "no one has yet found a way to drink for a living."

THE JOB SECURITY TROPHY

Looking for a career that will always be there, come inflation, depression, or revolution? Take this advice from writer Fay Weldon. "The chambermaid always survives the palace revolution. Someone has to make the beds."

THE MORNING COFFEE CUP:
FOR THE FACTORY WAKE-UP CALL

"One cannot walk through a mass-production factory," the poet W. H. Auden observed, "and not feel that one is in hell."

THERE WILL ALWAYS BE BUREAUCRATS MEDAL

★ **Third Place:** The Czars of Russia
"I do not rule Russia," Nicholas I, who was czar at the time, said. "Ten thousands clerks do."

★ **Runner-up:** Bureaucracy Is in the Eye of the Officeholder
Alben Barkley, as vice president for Harry Truman, knew a few things about bureaucrats, including the fact that there was an endless supply of politicians who wanted to become them.

"A bureaucrat," he said, "is a Democrat who holds some office that a Republican wants."

★ **And the Winner Is:** The Rocket Scientist
"We can lick gravity," said physicist Wernher von Braun, who designed America's first rocket program. "But sometimes the paperwork is overwhelming."

Chapter 10

The Everyday Awards: Creating the Extraordinary Out of the Ordinary

Life seems so ordinary on the average day. But any common moment can rise to the extraordinary with a bit of chance or unusual effort. That's how people get to live in newspaper houses, join the Smell Society, or dine at the elephant restaurant. And that's how anyone can win an Everyday Award.

SOMEONE PASS THE YAK BRICKS PRIZE: FOR ORIGINAL USE OF UNUSUAL BUILDING MATERIALS

★ **Third Place:** Coal

The Coal House of White Sulphur Springs, West Virginia, is the only residence in the world built entirely of coal.

★ **Runner-up:** Old Newspapers

The Newspaper House in Rockport, Massachusetts, was built 215 newspapers thick.

★ **And the Winner Is:** Tombstones

After the Civil War, O. E. Young built a two-story house in Petersburg, Virginia, by cementing together two thousand marble tombstones of Union soldiers killed in the siege of the town. The tombstones formed the walls, floor, and ceiling.

AND WHILE YOU'RE AT IT, PASS THE SOYBEANS AND SAWDUST PRIZE: FOR ORIGINAL USE OF ORDINARY STUFF WE'VE GOT TOO MUCH OF

★ **Third Place:** Driving the Bean

In the 1930s industrialist Henry Ford developed prototypes of a car to be built from soybeans.

★ **Runner-up:** Sailing the Ice

In the 1930s British inventor Geoffrey Pyke developed pykrete, a building material that was a mix of ice and sawdust.

He wanted the British Navy to build aircraft carriers out of pykrete for use in World War II. Test models actually stood up well to fire and under fire, but the ships were never built.

★ **And the Winner Is:** Flying the Boss

When Steady Ed Headrick died, he was cremated—but his ashes were not scattered. They were molded into a set of memorial-ashes flying disks.

Why? Steady Ed was one of those people not famous by name but famous by accomplishment. He invented the Frisbee and disk golf. Ed's memorial-ashes flying disks were given to family and friends.

THE ASSOCIATION OF ASSOCIATIONS JOINERS MEDAL:
FOR PEOPLE WHO PROVED THAT NOT ONLY IS THERE
SOMEPLACE FOR EVERYONE BUT THEY'RE ORGANIZED

★ **Third Place:** In the Halls

Just because you're not famous doesn't mean you can't be elected to a hall of fame. That's why third place ends up as an endless tie, this year among the Motorcycle Hall of Fame, Poker Hall of Fame, World Drum Corps Hall of Fame, Disco Dance Music Hall of Fame, and RV Hall of Fame.

★ **Runner-up:** The Filkers

The Filk Hall of Fame honors really special filkers, which is what it calls people who play science fiction folk music.

★ **And the Winner Is:** The Smellers

Writers George Bernard Shaw and H. G. Wells were founding members of the Smell Society, an English group dedicated to eliminating unpleasant odors.

THE NOSTALGICS UNANIMOUS PRIZE:
FOR MEMORIES THAT MAKE YOU SIGH

★ **Third Place:** The Five and Dime

When F. W. Woolworth opened his first variety store in 1879, every item in the shop sold for the same price—five cents.

Think of all the things you can buy for a nickel today. Well . . . um . . . there's a nickel; that still costs five cents.

★ **Runner-up:** Walden Pond

Writer Henry David Thoreau lived at Walden Pond for two years to immerse himself in the deep philosophy of the natural world. His stay cost him 27 cents a day. And they left the lights off for him.

★ **And the Winner Is:** The Phone

In the early 1900s, phone operators looked up numbers for callers, then hooked them up. The operators also gave folks the time of day and directions on how to get places. Plus, they'd take messages for you.

These services are now available again, but only a computer likes you enough to do all that for you. In the old days the services were provided by an actual human operator, who was often the nicest person you'd deal with all day.

THE BIG DEAL AWARDS:
FOR MAKING THEM OUT OF LITTLE DEALS

★ **Third Place:** The Vacuum Cleaner

When Hubert Booth of England developed the first workable vacuum cleaner in 1901, it was a huge device that required a horse and wagon to pull it through the streets and several men to operate it.

Still Booth's vacuum became a sensation after it was used to clean the carpets in Westminster Abbey for the coronation of King Edward VII.

Wealthy English women threw dirt parties so their friends could watch the carpets being vacuumed. Back then, people knew how to have fun.

★ **Runner-up:** The Restaurant

To attract tourists to Atlantic City in the years before casinos, a real estate speculator named James Lafferty built a six-story restaurant and hotel in the shape of an elephant named Lucy.

Customers climbed up spiral staircases inside Lucy's legs and sat in a dining room in her belly.

★ **And the Winner Is:** The Postmark

Each year thousands of people mail their valentines to Colorado, so they can be remailed from there to loved ones. Why? They want the special valentine postmark that only the town of Loveland, Colorado, can deliver.

THE MULTITASKING SPORTS AWARD:
FOR ATHLETES WHO DID THE EASY STUFF THE HARD WAY

★ **Third Place:** Not Your Mom's Apple Pie

Jimmy Wynn, the baseball slugger known as the Toy Cannon, took a common pregame meal and made it uncommon. Before each game, Wynn would eat steak and apple pie. Nothing unusual about that. But he'd eat them together—a piece of steak and a piece of pie in each mouthful.

Hitting a ball thrown by a major league pitcher is so tough that there's little a batter won't try to boost his confidence.

★ **Runner-up:** Coach and Ump

In an 1893 baseball game between Tulane and Louisiana State, T. L. Bayne coached both teams. He got no arguments because he also umped the game.

★ **And the Winner Is:** The Ball Hog

In 1935 running back J. Haines scored all the points for both teams during a football game between USC and the University of Washington.

Haines, who played for Washington, scored for USC when he was tackled in the end zone for a safety. Later in the game he ran a touchdown in for his own team. Final score: Washington 6, USC 2.

THE DOUBLE TROUBLE TROPHY:
AWARDED FOR MULTIPURPOSE CONCEPTS THAT ARE TWO, TWO, TWO TIMES AS USELESS AS ORDINARY BAD IDEAS

★ **Third Place:** On Land and in the Water

The Amphicar, built in the 1960s, could be driven right into the lake. Actually, you can drive any car into a lake. But this one you could drive back out again. Turn a switch and the car turned into a boat.

They only made one design mistake. Instead of combining the best features of a car and a boat, they ended up with an underpowered car that was also a tiny, cramped rocky boat.

★ **Runner-up:** The Mother and the Daughter

Irish poet William Butler Yeats proposed marriage to the Irish patriot Maud Gonne. When she turned him down, he proposed to Maud's daughter. She turned him down too.

★ **And the Winner Is:** Carmaker Henry Ford for Lifetime Achievements in Soybeans

Ford, a champion of the common bean that won't quit, once served a sixteen-course meal made entirely from soybeans. He also had a suit and tie made from soy cloth and experimented with making a car from soybeans.

THE GOING TO THE DOGS PRIZE:
FOR FAMOUS PEOPLE WITH SURPRISING THOUGHTS ABOUT DOGS

★ **Third Place:** Writer Aldous Huxley

"To his dog, every man is Napoleon," Huxley said. "Hence, the constant popularity of dogs."

★ **Runner-up:** Writer Robert Benchley

The Algonquin Round Table wit was questioned about the value of getting a dog as a pet for a child. Benchley observed that "a dog teaches a boy fidelity, perseverance and to turn around three times before lying down."

★ **And the Winner Is:** Playwright August Strindberg

"I loathe people who keep dogs," Strindberg sneered. "They are cowards who haven't got the guts to bite people themselves."

THE GARDEN VARIETY AWARDS:
FOR PLANTS NAMED AFTER PEOPLE EVEN
THOUGH THEY SOUND LIKE THEY WEREN'T

★ **Third Place:** Macadamia Nuts
Named for John McAdam.

★ **Runner-up:** Dahlias
Named for Anders Dahl.

★ **And the Winner Is:** Zinnias
Named for Johann Zinn.

THE EVERYDAY POLITICAL TROPHIES:
FOR POLITICIANS WHO REALIZE THAT
NO MOVE IS INSIGNIFICANT IF THEY CAN
POSSIBLY GET SOME ADVANTAGE OUT OF IT

★ **Third Place:** The Folksy Presidents

What did presidents Richard Nixon and Gerald Ford have in common?

No, not that they were both Republicans connected by Watergate—which undid one and helped the other become a stock character on *Saturday Night Live*.

They shared another habit with many Americans, but ones who lived in less-pressured situations. As presidents, both Nixon and Ford claimed that each day they read the sports pages first.

Nixon said this to show the American people his more human face. Ford said it because he actually did read the sports pages first each morning. So it's either a folksy touch or two presidents who weren't taking care of business.

★ **Runner-up:** The Wallflowers

When the Twist became a dance craze in the 1960s, it not only shocked parents around America, it shocked governments. Oddly enough the dance was condemned by all sides—the Catholic Church in New York, Communist officials in China and East Germany, and the anti-Communist government in South Vietnam.

Authorities who were against each other were united by one thing: they didn't like the Twist. Ordinary people? They kept dancing.

★ **And the Winner Is:** The Golfer

When Ferdinand Marcos ruled the Philippines, his bodyguards would line the fairways whenever he played golf. They were there to protect their president from dangerous enemies—like his golf partners.

The bodyguards also made sure Marcos never hooked or sliced. All his drives ended up straight down the fairway and, no matter who he was playing, farther along than the competition.

THE EMPTY PROMISES PRIZE:
FOR UNUSUAL POLITICS AS USUAL

★ **Third Place:** Support Education, Yeah, Right

Elected officials brag about their support for education. They're all in favor of it.

If so many politicians really supported education, why aren't our teachers better paid and our students better educated?

Politicians know that if more people were educated they wouldn't keep falling for the same phony promises from the same double-talking politicians.

Practically no one in America is literate in the old English sense. In eighteenth-century England an illiterate was someone with an insufficient knowledge of ancient Greek and Latin.

★ **Runner-up:** Vote Early, Vote Often

A farmer in Newmarket, England, registered two of her cows to vote in local elections in 2004. She listed the cows on the voter registration form as Henry and Sophie Bull.

The year before, she had registered Jake Woofles to vote. Woofles turned out to be a dog. Election officials denied the animals the right to vote, even though a clear case could be made that the country had already gone to the dogs.

★ **And the Winner Is:** Democrats Are People Too

You say there's no difference between Democrats and Republicans? The survey says that Democrats jog more than Republicans, smoke less than Republicans, and a higher percentage of black homosexuals are Democrats than are white homosexuals.

THE GREAT FAILURE PRIZE:
FOR FAMOUS PEOPLE WHO DIDN'T
START OUT LOOKING LIKE WINNERS

★ **Third Place:** Charles Darwin

Before he made one of the world's great breakthroughs in science, Darwin flunked out of university twice—from Edinburgh, where he studied medicine, and from Cambridge, where he studied for the priesthood.

Darwin shipped out on the HMS *Beagle* on a whim and to get away from a disapproving father. He returned from that journey as a great biology researcher and eventually caused a revolution in how we think about man's place in nature.

★ **Runner-up:** Auguste Rodin

The would-be artist flunked the entrance exam to France's prestigious art school, the École des Beaux-Arts. He took the exam a second time and flunked that too.

After flunking a third time, Rodin sat and thought about his future. Then he stopped taking exams and went on to become one of the world's greatest sculptors.

★ **And the Winner Is:** Guiseppe Verdi

The composer-in-training was rejected by Italy's great music school, the Milan Conservatorium, because the teachers judged him to have no musical talent. Besides, they thought he didn't look like a musician.

Without talent or looks, Verdi went on to become one of the greatest composers of all time.

THE FLORENCE SOCIETY HONORS:
GO TO FLORENCE

Florence Nightingale was an inspiration to millions, a nurse hailed as a savior for her devotion to the sick, the injured, and the wounded in war.

When she finally retired after fifty-five years of service, Nightingale received a unique honor: a letter of tribute signed by thousands of women whose parents had named them Florence in her honor.

Chapter 11

The Spin Awards:
Fooling Most of the People
Enough of the Time

In the world before public relations, Nebraska was called the Bug-Eating State and Missouri was nicknamed the Puke State.

Apply a little Chamber of Commerce PR and you have Nebraska, the Cornhusker State, and Missouri, the Show-Me State.

Without the benefits of advertising, we'd still be eating bugs and sending them right back up again. With PR spin, we've got places to go on the family vacation.

When advertisers spend fortunes to promote their products and services, they expect to win a few awards along with our hearts and most of our money. And they do win prizes because they give them to themselves, like the Web Awards, which honor spin artists who could make spiders jealous.

THE WEB AWARDS

THE BLACK WIDOW'S WEB

A U.S. airline redefined a plane crash as an "involuntary conversion of a 727."

THE HEALTH CARE WEB

English hospital administrators asked their doctors to stop talking about patients dying, instead referencing "negative patient care outcomes."

THE WEB OF POWER

Iranian President Mohammad Khatami explained the arrest of a leader of the opposition party in 1998: "No viewpoints are banned except those banned by the law."

THE WEB OF INSIDERS

In the 1980s the Argentine government maintained a policy that allowed them to rename Indians if they had Indian names that sounded foreign to the government officials who kept the records.

These Indians were descended from the land's original inhabitants, giving a new twist to the meaning of "foreigner" as anyone who isn't running the place at the time.

THE WEB OF THE ELITE

In 1995 Stanford University administrators decided to consolidate the school's image message. They asked professors to use one of six adjectives whenever they referred to the school in public or in press talking points.

Which adjectives? "Incomparable, challenging, vibrant." Those were the three that made a kind of sense if you were a paid Stanford booster.

The other three adjectives were also intended to promote the school. So let's try them out.

"Stanford is a boundless school." Well, it does have a large campus.

"Stanford is a stunning university." I've known stunning women who went to Stanford. But have you ever been stunned by a school? Maybe if you ran into the Cardinal defensive line—in a good year.

Finally, the professors might have said, "Stanford is a Western school." Which demonstrates that facts are often the dullest of your choices.

THE WEB OF MANIFEST DESTINY

During the September Massacres of 1792, French revolutionaries slaughtered anyone who was insufficiently revolutionary in their fervor and insufficiently slow on their feet.

When leaders of other European nations objected to the bloody excesses, the revolutionary visionary Georges Jacques Danton explained that the killings were an "unavoidable sacrifice."

Government leaders have been making unavoidable sacrifices of their enemies ever since. Prior to Danton's spin gem, they simply murdered them.

THE LEMON WEB

Citrus growers use ethylene oxide to turn lemons yellow after they're picked because citrus doesn't ripen once it's off the tree. This process used to be called gassing until growers decided that didn't sound consumer-friendly.

They didn't change the ripening process. They changed the name, to curing or de-greening.

THE FAT WEB

The Southern California burger chain Fatburger went after diet-conscious fast-food fans with a low-fat fatburger. Made, no doubt, with heart-healthy grease.

THE WEB OF PRIVILEGE

"Misdemeanor murder" was what some police departments in the South called murders of black people by other blacks in the years before the Civil Rights movement straightened them out.

THE WEB OF CLARITY

A Lake Tahoe resident told a *Saturday Evening Post* reporter that the lake was so clear you could see a beer can forty feet down.

THE WEB OF THE WHITE HOUSE

In 2003 Secretary of Defense Donald Rumsfeld told the press: "As we know, there are known knowns; there are things we know we know. We also know there are known unknowns; that is to say we know there are some things we do not know. But there are also unknown unknowns—the ones we don't know we don't know."

THE WEB OF HARD CASH

You and I can't get enough cash, but there was a time when we couldn't get any. Cash in eighteenth-century England meant gold, not bills.

Paper money was accepted by English merchants only because the government guaranteed that people could convert it into cash (or gold) whenever they wanted.

Fear of a French invasion at the end of the eighteenth century sent the Brits into a financial panic. People stormed the banks demanding what they thought of as cash for what we now think of as cash. They didn't want paper. They wanted the gold.

The banks didn't have enough gold to go around, and the government wouldn't allow British banks to be ruined by this gold rush. So for twenty years the British money supply was all paper. To help people accept the idea of paper currency, they started calling it cash, just like gold.

THE WEB OF UNREAL ESTATE

The U.S. government cheated the Mesquakie Indians in ways they didn't even think of cheating other tribes.

When the Mesquakie got tired of having their land taken away by white settlers in 1856, the Indians took all their money and bought some land in Iowa, just like the white people did. Government officials then declared that Indians couldn't own land because legally they weren't people.

The Leftover Spin Awards honor the only advertising and PR campaigns that did not win other awards.

THE CIGARETTE WARS MEDAL OF HONOR

★ **Third Place:** The Weight-Loss Program

During the Irish famine of the nineteenth century, many people starved because the poorhouses set up to feed them wouldn't admit smokers and tobacco addicts would rather starve than give up their habit.

★ **Runner-up:** The Smokeless Smokes

In the 1970s tobacco companies wouldn't admit that cigarettes would make you sick if not dead. But this position of denial didn't stop them from trying to market healthy cigarettes.

R. J. Reynolds came up with an all-natural smoke called Real in the seventies, then a smokeless cigarette called Premier in the eighties. The company spent $300 million promoting the two brands.

Execs had everything figured out except for one thing: why would people who smoked be concerned about their health? Both brands were consumer flops.

★ **And the Winners Are:** The Smoking Grammarians

In the 1950s Americans rose in protest against the evil perpetrated by two cigarette brands: Winston and Tareyton.

People weren't upset because cigarettes were soft machines that would kill you and make you smell bad first. And they weren't protesting that cigarettes were the drug of choice among teenagers.

What upset them? Bad English. As in the two ad slogans:

1. "Winston tastes good like a cigarette should."

2. "Us Tareyton smokers would rather fight than switch."

People, they felt, should be able to smoke themselves to death grammatically.

THE NON-PC ADVERTISING AWARD:
FOR OLD AD CAMPAIGNS THEY'D NEVER RUN TODAY

★ **Third Place:** The Swamp Campaign

Florida's Cypress Knee Museum used this roadside sign to attract tourists: LADY, IF HE WON'T STOP HIT HIM ON THE HEAD WITH YOUR SHOE.

If tourists did stop at the museum, they would see truncated limbs of swamp cypress trees that were shaped into the image of animals and famous people.

★ **Runner-up:** The Sideshow Promotion

The Ringling Brothers Circus once used this pitch to get people to come see the circus fat lady, the five-hundred-pound Alice from Dallas: "It took two men to hug her and ten men to lug her."

★ **And the Winner Is:** The Uplifting Drink

In the 1920s, 7-Up was sold as an antidepressant. It contained lithium. The 7-Up slogan: "Take the ouch out of grouch."

Anyone know what they expected you to do with the leftover "gr"?

CELEBRITY SPOKESMAN WANNA-BE TROPHY

President Theodore Roosevelt was visiting Nashville, where he drank a local blend of coffee. He enjoyed it so much, Roosevelt commented, "It's good to the last drop."

And that's how Maxwell House got its famous advertising slogan—for free and from a president.

THE BACKFIRE PRIZE:
FOR AD CAMPAIGNS WITH SURPRISING RESULTS

Companies want their products to become popular, but they don't want the registered names of their products to become too popular. If a trademarked name becomes part of the ordinary language, the company can lose the trademark.

Happened to Aladdin Industries, which made the original Thermos bottle, when the word "Thermos" was a registered trademark. The company helped lose that trademark with an ad campaign that declared "Thermos is a household word."

Once it achieved that status, competitors were free to use the word "thermos" in their own ads. Oops.

MOST NAUSEATING PR CAMPAIGN

When United began its first passenger flights—a five-stop hop from Oakland to Cheyenne, Wyoming—the airline wanted to reassure customers that they'd be well looked after because each Air Hostess was also a registered nurse.

Instead, having nurses on board reminded nervous first-timers that flying might make them sick to their stomach.

BEST EDUCATIONAL ADVERTISING

The modern supermarket was invented in 1915 when Clarence Saunders opened the first Piggly Wiggly markets in Tennessee. Why did he choose that unusual name? "So people will ask that very question," Saunders explained.

THE ANTIDISCRIMINATION
PURPLE PEOPLE PR PRIZE

In 1997 a Teletubbies marketing exec explained why the TV show featured a purple Teletubby: "In life, there are all colors, and the Teletubbies are a reflection of that."

While people come in some colors, purple isn't ordinarily one of them.

THE TWO-SECOND PROMOTION PRIZE

To advertise Arnold Schwarzenegger's summer movie *Last Action Hero*, Columbia Pictures negotiated with NASA to paint the movie logo on the side of a rocket for its next launch. The cost: $500,000. The payoff: Arnie would get to push the launch button.

The deal fell through at the last moment. So did the movie, which was a bomb. As for Schwarzenegger, he had to settle for becoming governor of California.

THE UNINTENDED ADVERTISING AWARD

Laugh In was such a popular TV show in the sixties that when they started using the punch line, "Look that up in your Funk and Wagnall's," sales of the dictionary shot up.

Great Moments in the Downward Advancement of the Human Race, Forget-Me-Not Division

Companies spend millions to get their ad slogans to linger in the mind so that when you want a soda, you don't think of all the interesting alternatives—you just grab a Coke.

Who can forget the tag lines for these familiar products? Most of us, that's who. See if you can match the one-time ad slogan with the still famous product.

The Products

Coca-Cola

McDonald's

Lifesavers

Cadillac

Kellogg's Corn Flakes

Post's Grape-Nuts

Dr. Hitchcock's Kickapoo Oil

Fletcher's Castoria Oil

Gold Medal Flour

Kodak

The Slogans

The penalty for leadership.

We do it all for you.

Eventually. Why not now.

Good for man or beast.

Children cry for it.

You press the button. We do the rest.

There's a reason.

America's waking thought.

For that stormy breath.

The intellectual beverage and temperance drink.

The Answers

The penalty for leadership: Cadillac.

We do it all for you: McDonald's.

Eventually. Why not now: Gold Medal Flour.

Good for man or beast: Dr. Hitchcock's Kickapoo Oil.

Children cry for it: Fletcher's Castoria Oil.

You press the button. We do the rest: Kodak.

There's a reason: Post's Grape-Nuts.

America's waking thought: Kellogg's Corn Flakes.

For that stormy breath: Lifesavers.

The intellectual beverage and temperance drink: Coca-Cola.

MOVING THE MERCHANDISE MEDAL:
FOR PRODUCTS THAT WERE HOT, THEN WERE NOT, AND NOW LOOK KIND OF SILLY

★ **Third Place:** The Princess

The Princess phone was sold in the 1950s as the perfect phone for teenage girls because it was small and lightweight. Girls could handle the Princess without straining their pretty little arm muscles.

The Princess was actually bigger and heavier than the cell phones now used by manly callers.

★ **Runner-up:** The $1.25 Dress

Scott Paper had a lot of paper on its hands in the 1960s, so the company came up with a line of paper dresses for only $1.25 each, sold on the wear-it-and-throw-it-away plan.

Paper dresses led to paper bikinis and even paper wedding gowns. Why aren't people wearing paper clothes anymore? Because while people will follow a stupid fad, they won't follow it forever.

★ **And the Winner Is:** The Phone Reservation

AT&T was ahead of its time in the 1960s when the company tried to sell the public on a picture phone.

There were a few drawbacks. You had to go to an AT&T office to use the phone. The person you were calling had to go to another office at a prearranged time. This meant, you had to make reservations to make a phone call. And pay a premium. Who could turn down a deal like that? Just about everybody.

Dulling the Competitive Edge Prize

Just because the competition does something dumb, there's no reason you can't do it too. That's why the prizewinner is a tie between Coke and Pepsi.

Coca-Cola came out with New Coke in 1982. People hated it, saying no to the New. Diehards rushed to hoard old Coke so they would have something left to drink in the New Coke world.

Coke surrendered to popular revulsion and went back to using the old formula. But not before Pepsi had a good laugh at watching Coke forced to eat the soda no one would drink. Then Pepsi came out with its own downer in 1992.

Crystal Pepsi tasted like regular Pepsi but looked like water. They'd taken the color out. What worked for 7-Up—the appearance of clarity—didn't work for Pepsi. The public response was clear—they didn't want clear cola any more than they wanted a new one.

THE PET STICK TROPHY:
FOR WACKY IDEAS THAT COULD HAVE BECOME AS BIG A FAD AS OTHER WACKY IDEAS, BUT DIDN'T

★ **Third Place:** Underwear Vending Machines

Macys tried them out in the sixties, and plenty of people dropped into the store to see the machines in action. Only problem was they were rarely in action.

No one wanted to buy undershorts from a rude machine, which wasn't any faster than buying shorts from a rude sales clerk.

★ **Runner-up:** The Pilot Car

In redesigning the 1962 Avanti, Studebaker put the dashboard controls overhead on the roof so the driver could feel like a pilot.

But drivers didn't want to feel like pilots. They wanted to feel like drivers. The car flopped.

★ **And the Winner Is:** The Whiskey Tender

In the 1960s an English company placed a new kind of vending machine in London tube stations. People dropped in a few coins and received a cup of whiskey and soda. The machine had a clock to turn itself off during hours when pubs were closed. But the public turned off the idea instead.

THE NAME THAT PRODUCT PRIZE

Big companies spend millions coming up with names for their new products and corporate identities—sometimes creating the most expensive laughs in history.

★ **Third Place:** The Chevy Nova

Chevy execs were surprised when the Nova didn't sell well in Latin America. Then they found out why. In Spanish *no va* means "does not go."

★ **Runner-up:** Standard Oil

The gas giant planned to change its corporate name to Enco, but reconsidered when it learned that in Japanese *enco* meant "car that does not go."

★ **And the Winner Is:** United Airlines

In 1987 United changed its company name to Allegis. Spent millions to do it.

Then it cost the company millions more to change the name back to United Airlines a few months later. Customers wanted to fly United, not Allegis. The business world had a good laugh at a corporation that spent so much money just to end up exactly where they would have been if they'd left it alone.

Great, If Brief, Moments on the Shelf, for Products that Never Quite Took Off

1. The don't-fall-asleep-at-the-wheel hat. If you nodded off and hit your head on the steering wheel, a hat alarm buzzed—which would wake you up just in time to see that tree hit your car.

2. Moon-landing gum balls with a moonlike cratered surface, to celebrate Apollo 11's landing on the moon.

3. People Crackers for Dogs. The reverse of Animal Crackers, each box contained bite-sized dogcatchers and mailmen.

4. An electric spaghetti fork that automatically wound up the noodles for you.

5. Toaster bacon. For some reason, people in the sixties didn't want to drop slices of bacon, wrapped in foil, into their toasters.

6. The patient doll. Girls have gone for dolls they can dress, dolls they can burp, dolls that cry and drool. But they got turned off by Marybel, the sick doll that came with its own measles, cast, and crutches.

7. The twistfurter, a hot dog with a twisted middle. Why would you want a twisted frankfurter? Because back in the sixties you couldn't stop dancing the Twist, could you?

Chapter 12

Champion Fighters, Davids, and Whiners

There are two fighting impulses: to crush the opposition or whine them into submission. If neither tactic works, there's always the David approach to Goliaths—stand back, throw a few stones, and if you get a lucky hit, claim quick victory before the big guy gets up again.

However they fight their battles, they're all champions here.

THE BILLY MARTIN MEMORIAL DIRT-KICKING TROPHY

Given for exemplary bad sportsmanship to athletes who got the last laugh by following the principles of a manager whose challenge to umpires everywhere was: If you don't want me kicking the dirt, why don't you move home plate into the grass?

★ **Third Place:** The Champ

Heavyweight boxing champion Jack Johnson proved that the race wasn't over just because you've lost.

While in Australia, Johnson accepted a challenge to race a kangaroo. But Johnson didn't know what the Australians knew: kangaroos are faster than people—in the sprints.

Johnson lost the race. But he kept chasing the kangaroo past the finish line. He ran it so hard and long that the kangaroo dropped over dead.

★ **Runner-up:** The Sultan

Baseball great Babe Ruth was a fan favorite, so popular that he had the Yankees install a large trash basket next to his locker—into which all his fan mail was dumped unread.

★ **And the Winner Is:** The Emperor

Chinese Emperor Wen Ti proved that chess can be a physically challenging sport. The ancient emperor learned the game by watching two chess experts play. He was outraged to see that royalty had been reduced to pieces in a game. So he had the players' heads cut off.

THE DUMB JOCK AWARD: FOR GUYS WHO PROVE THEY DON'T CALL THEM DUMB JOCKS FOR NOTHING

During Strike Out Against Domestic Violence Night at a minor league baseball stadium in 1994, both dugouts emptied as players from the Durham Bulls and the Winston-Salem Warthogs fought in a half-hour brawl over a beaning.

Ten players were thrown out of the game. One Warthog ended up in the hospital with serious injuries. But at least their violence was public, not domestic.

Odd Enemies Ribbon: Given to combatants who might have made better allies

In the Battle of New Orleans during the War of 1812, Andrew Jackson led a citizen coalition against the regular British army—and destroyed them, to the great surprise of the British generals.

Jackson's troops included pirates, frontiersmen, and the free black men of New Orleans. The former slaves fought on the side of slave owners like Jackson against the British, who might have freed the slaves of the South if they had won the battle and the war.

REAL WORLD CHAMPIONS

Sugar Ray Robinson, Muhammad Ali, Sugar Ray Leonard. Great champions, but could they hold their own with these world-class fighting champs?

World Champion in the Woolly-Weight Division: The big horns

Bighorn sheep, which take up to eight years to grow a set of those curled horns, have such hard skulls they can butt heads for hours. They don't hurt themselves even though they ram together at twenty mph.

Oddly, males will only fight in their own weight class against other males who have the same horn size.

Mussel-Weight Champ: Mussels

Those masses of mussels you see clinging to the rocks at the seashore are nearly defenseless against all the tide-pool shoppers looking for a free lunch.

But when a sea snail crawls onto the mass to pry open mussel shells, the mussels net the snail, lassoing it with the same filaments they use to stick to the rocks. If they are successful, the predator becomes the prey. They have yet to snare a human hunter this way.

SUB-FLYWEIGHT CHAMP: THE MOSQUITO

America is heir to the mosquito. Without that bloodsucker, we'd have a much smaller country or speak French.

In 1802 the French sent an army of 33,000 troops to protect their vast territory in the southern region of North America. The mosquitoes defeated the French (well, who hasn't?), spreading yellow fever that killed 29,000 troops.

As a result, France agreed to the Louisiana Purchase, selling off half of America at a bargain-basement price, feeling it got the better of the deal.

Congress should have rewarded our ally by naming the mosquito our national symbol, for patriotic contributions above and beyond any services provided by the bald eagle.

TWO-SPORT CHAMP: THE MAT MEN

Boxers vs. wrestlers—who'd win?

1913: Boxer Jack Johnson knocked out single-named Liberian wrestler Spoul in Paris.

1921: Wrestler Farmer Burns pinned boxer Billy Papke in Reno, Nevada.

1922: Wrestler Strong Boy Price pinned boxer Sailor Adams in Joplin, Missouri.

1922: Heavyweight champ Jack Dempsey and wrestling champion Ed "Strangler" Lewis milked the idea of a showdown match for months. They got a lot of publicity, but never got into the ring to fight it out.

1976: Heavyweight champ Muhammad Ali and Japanese wrestling king Antonio Inoki fought to a draw in Tokyo. Inoki employed the martial arts tactic of lying on his back and kicking whenever Ali got close, which wasn't often.

1976: Wrestler Andre the Giant mauled heavyweight boxer Chuck Wepner and won the match by tossing him out of the ring.

Totals: Wrestlers win, 3-1-1 (with one no-show).

FLYWEIGHT CHAMP: THE ACE

The notorious Red Baron, the German ace of World War I, was a fighter pilot of immense talent and ego, inflated by a string of eighty successful dogfights.

"When I have shot down an Englishman," he boasted, "my hunting passion is satisfied for a quarter of an hour."

No word on how long his passion was satisfied if he shot down a Frenchman or American.

BOOK-WEIGHT CHAMP: THE READER

Some people still think we need a good reason to go to war. But history shows us that just about any excuse will do.

In the sixth century the Irish warrior Columba copied a manuscript without first obtaining the owner's permission. This led to a war called the Battle of the Book, in which three thousand soldiers were slaughtered over the protection of intellectual property rights.

BARE KNUCKLE CHAMPS: THE EMBARRASSMENTS

The first professional American boxers were ex-slaves Bill Richmond and Tom Molineaux, but they didn't fight in America. Instead, their managers took them to England, where they fought on the professional circuit of the early 1800s, drawing huge crowds because they were Americans and black.

Because of English prejudice against blacks, their white opponents had to fight them under assumed names.

FAKE-WEIGHT CHAMP: THE MOVIE DIRECTOR

Movie stars may get into hundreds of fights and never lose—until the real thing comes along.

Star Henry Fonda and director John Ford were old friends, so you'd think they'd have a good time making *Mister Roberts*, with Fonda in the title role he'd played on the stage.

Didn't work. When Fonda refused to play the role Ford's way, the director punched out his star. They managed to finish the film, but it finished their friendship too.

THE DAVID SOCIETY'S ONE MORE GOLIATH BITES THE DUST PRIZE:

Perpetuates the notion that even though the smart money is always on the big guy, the little guy will win just often enough to stay in the game

THE BEN & JERRY ICE CREAM PRIZE:
GOES TO JERRY AND BEN

The folksy ice cream nuts from Burlington, Vermont, became the talk of the town when they opened a single small store in the 1970s. But they wanted to go national.

When Ben and Jerry tried to sell their ice cream to supermarkets, they were shut out by the dominant force in upscale ice cream, Häagen-Dazs, a Bronx, New York, company now owned by Pillsbury.

The Häagen-Dazs people told stores if they added Ben & Jerry's ice cream to their freezers, they wouldn't be allowed to sell Häagen-Dazs anymore. Tough luck was the basic message the stores had for Ben & Jerry.

But the little guys struck back with an anticorporate PR campaign that got ice-cream lovers across the nation asking, "What's the Doughboy afraid of?"

Battered by too much bad publicity, Häagen-Dazs surrendered and moved over on the shelf. That's why when you go to the store, you now have a choice of how you will completely blow your diet.

THE SWARM, TINY DAVIDS, SWARM AWARD:
GOES TO THE MILLIPEDES

In the late 1800s there was a sudden upsurge in the millipede population west of the Mississippi. But those leggy little crawlers couldn't stand up to the tough cowboys, pioneers, and gunslingers who ruled the Wild West—could they?

The millipedes swarmed over railroad tracks, crushed by the thousands under the iron wheels of progress. Millipede slime grew so thick on the tracks that they caused train derailments. The rails had to be covered with sand so the train wheels could maintain traction.

THE HIGH STAKES AWARD:
FOR CLEVER USE OF VOLCANOES

When Roman authorities attempted to burn St. Agatha at the stake in the year 251, their fire was doused by a volcanic eruption.

But as often happens to Davids after their moment of triumph, the Goliaths had the last say. They beheaded St. Agatha as soon as the volcano let up.

THE I CANNOT TELL TOO MANY LIES TROPHY

How come we haven't had another politician named Honest Anybody since Honest Abe?

In America anyone can rise from poverty to become president of the United States—as long as they can raise $200 million for the ad campaign. But while we're likely to face a long stretch of President Goliaths, that doesn't stop the Davids from entering the race.

★ **Third Place:** The Surprise Candidate
In 1940 the Surprise Party nominated a surprising candidate to run against Franklin Roosevelt: comedienne Gracie Allen of Burns and Allen fame. She lost.

★ **Runner-up:** The Lazy Candidate
Folksinger Utah Phillips ran for president on the Sloth and Indolence ticket. He lost.

★ **And the Winner Is:** The Stag Candidate
TV comedian Pat Paulsen ran for president in 1968, heading the ticket of the Straight-Talking American Government Party. His campaign promise? "I know what the average American wants. In fact, I'd like to get a little of it myself."

THE COUNTER-ANTIESTABLISHMENT PRIZE: GOES TO THE ESTABLISHMENT

The noble concept that the truth shall set you free has been trumped throughout history by the corollary that the truth shall get you in big trouble with the authorities.

This award honors the authorities who stood up against the truth, suppressing it in the name of maintaining beliefs that we now laugh at as ridiculous.

★ Third Place: The Theoretician

During the Dark and semidim Middle Ages, the Vatican establishment held that the Earth was the center of the universe. But the Polish astronomer Copernicus reasoned that the Earth wasn't even the center of our solar system. The sun was.

Copernicus couldn't prove his assertion because he didn't have a telescope, which Galileo later used to back up this theory.

That shortsightedness was good enough for the Church, whose leaders argued that Copernicus had been merely doing an exercise in theoretical math and his calculations had nothing to do with reality.

★ Runner-up: The Priest

Copernicus got off lightly. In the sixteenth century, an Italian priest named Giordano Bruno figured out that the universe must contain many other suns and planets—but we couldn't see them because they were too far away.

These views so angered the Vatican authorities that they had Bruno burned at the stake.

★ And the Winner Is: The Astronomer

Bruno's punishment so intimidated Galileo that the astronomer recanted the telescopic evidence he had gathered that Copernicus was right and the sun was at the center of our solar system.

When the truth is controlled by authorities who don't want to hear the facts, then seeing is not believing. The executioner's ax is believing.

Church leaders finally came around and saw the folly of their predecessors' ways. They pardoned Galileo for his crimes—in 1992, more than 350 years after the fact.

Mom's Spirit Award: For building the competitive edge among young Davids

★ **Third Place:** The Knockdown Artist

"Burly" Early Wynn was a tough pitcher for the Cleveland Indians who would throw at a batter's head if he was crowding the plate. Asked if he would throw at his own mother, Wynn admitted, "I'd have to. Mom was a pretty good curveball hitter."

★ **Runner-up:** The Writer

"If a writer has to rob his mother, he will not hesitate," novelist William Faulkner boasted. "The 'Ode on a Grecian Urn' is worth any number of old ladies."

★ **And the Winner Is:** The Lip

Leo Durocher was tough as a baseball player, tougher still as manager of the New York Giants. He explained his infield defense this way: "If my own mother's coming home with the winning run, I trip her up," the Lip said. "Afterward, I'd say, 'Mom, I'm sorry.' And I truly am. But even my own mother doesn't get to score the winning run that beats me."

THE ALMOST DAVID TROPHY:
GOES TO THE BOOMERANG SAINTS

When nonbelievers attempted to martyr the saints Cosmas and Damian, the brothers used their spiritual power to turn around the arrows and rocks, and fly them back at their persecutors.

However, they had no such power over being beheaded, which they were.

THE WHINER AWARDS

God lets whiners live longer because people who complain a lot understand how the system works.

We live in a whining culture where the people in power whine even more than the whiners who want to become the people in power. And even though they win the Whiner Awards, they probably think the trophies aren't big enough.

TOO MANY BELLS PRIZE

In 1981 an Italian court rejected a petition from the whining family of the Duke of Gualtieri, who wanted him to stop ringing the bell of his private chapel every time he had sex.

The tintinnabulation of the bells, bells, bells was making them crazy.

TOO MUCH SLAMMING PRIZE

The people who ran college basketball banned the slam dunk in 1968 because they thought it improper behavior that would compromise the higher standards of the game.

You might figure that rule would last about thirty seconds into the first game a star athlete like Kareem Abdul-Jabbar played. But the ban was stubbornly kept in place until 1976 before college authorities came to their senses and decided it was actually okay if basketball was exciting.

Too Bald and Shrunken Prize

St. Albert the Great, one of history's first scientists, maintained that men would grow bald if they engaged in too much sex—instantly making baldness the number-one hair style in Europe.

Albert also believed that sex caused your brain to shrink. He further theorized that women were not as moral as men because they contained more liquid, which takes "things up easily and holds on to them poorly."

Too Much Existence Prize

Lewis Carroll conceived one of the most entrancing fantasy worlds in *Alice in Wonderland*, but found it difficult to get along in the mundane world.

"In some ways people who don't exist are nicer than people who do," he complained, even though he himself did exist.

Too Many Headaches Prize

If anyone in the court of Ivan the Terrible complained of headaches, the Russian czar ordered his soldiers to drive a nail into the sufferer's head. This didn't cure the headache, but it did stop the complaining.

Too Much Paper Prize

In the Dark Ages while the countries of Europe used gold and silver coins as their currency, the Chinese government created paper money to replace the country's popular bronze coins.

How did the emperor and his court get merchants throughout China to agree that worthless paper signed by government officials would now carry the weight of valuable metals? No whining, the emperor decreed. The army executed anyone who complained.

The Six Cents Is Too High a Price Prize

Baseball players and umps have been sniping at each other longer and harder than refs and athletes from other sports. Maybe it's because they have too much time on their hands during the gaps while the ball is not in play.

How long has this been going on? In one of the first professional games in 1846 between the New Yorkers and the Knickerbockers, one of the players got fined for arguing with the ump over a call. The fine? Six cents.

The price of baseball whining has inflated since then, along with the price of bleacher seats, ball park hot dogs, and switch-hitting center fielders. Now a player wouldn't even snivel for under a thousand.

THE PRESIDENT OF THE
WHINING STATES OF AMERICA PRIZE

During Franklin Roosevelt's reign, the White House kitchen was ruled by a cook who served so much chicken that chicken fatigue set in among the West Wing's regular diners. FDR sent a note of complaint to his wife about the food.

"I am getting to the point," the president wrote to Eleanor, "where my stomach positively rebels, and this does not help my relations with foreign powers. I bit two of them today."

By the way, what whine did presidents Franklin Roosevelt and George Bush the First have in common?

They both hated broccoli when it was served at White House dinners over their objections.

Chapter 13

World Class Unlucky

The French writer Jean Cocteau had a clear understanding of the value of luck. "How else," he pondered, "do you explain the success of those you don't like."

Then there's bad luck, of which most of us have had our share. (If by some chance you haven't had yours, send a self-addressed envelope; you're welcome to some of mine.)

And if you're feeling exceptionally plagued, you can enter the next round of the World's Unluckiest Contest and see if you can top these losing winners.

UNLUCKY IN LOVE

The Neiman Marcus Department Store, which caters to the exclusive tastes of the wealthy, thought it a polite gesture to send thank-you notes to men who had purchased particularly valuable jewelry.

But the store sent the notes to the men's home addresses, where the letters were opened by wives for whom that valuable jewelry had not necessarily been purchased.

Unlucky in Hair

The Greek playwright Aeschylus was killed when a tortoise fell on his head. The tortoise had been carried aloft by an eagle, which apparently thought Aeschylus's bald head was a rock it could smash the turtle upon.

Unlucky at Breakfast

In the 1800s a German traveler in Africa was killed by tribal warriors for the sin of having eggs for breakfast.

This particular tribe had a peculiar belief. They considered eggs a kind of Pandora's Box, containers of mysterious, untapped powers that man would be wise not to unleash by having breakfast. That German traveler would have been wise to consider the noncontroversial spirituality of oatmeal.

Unlucky in Russia

Czar Ivan became the emperor of Russia as an infant in 1740. He was overthrown when he was three months old, before he really got rolling.

UNLUCKIEST CRUSADER

In the thirteenth century a shepherd boy known as Stephen of Vendome led fifty thousand children on a march across France to the sea, promising that they would free the Holy Land from the Muslims.

Why would unarmed children succeed in a crusade where the mounted knights and piked armies of Europe had failed? Because the children were sinless, according to Stephen.

As it turned out, the young crusaders were definitely more sinned against than sinning. When the Children's Crusade reached the Mediterranean—which Stephen predicted would part for them like the Red Sea for Moses—they were abducted by traders and sold into slavery in Egypt.

UNLUCKY IN MAGNETISM

By the time they plummet through the Earth's atmosphere and smash into the ground, most meteorites have burned down to pebble size. So people are rarely hurt by collision with space debris.

History records the human death toll from hit-by-a-meteorite as zero.

But an Egyptian dog was killed by a meteorite in 1911. And then in 1954 an Alabama woman was injured when a meteorite crashed through the roof of her house.

UNLUCKIEST FREEDOM FIGHTER

Louis XV, king of France, became convinced that those brash American colonials had a chance to defeat the British in their Revolutionary War. So he emptied much of his country's treasury to send them guns and supplies.

With French help, the Americans won their freedom. But the French aristocracy lost their heads. Louis's efforts to fund the American Revolution impoverished his own realm and eventually led to the French Revolution.

UNLUCKIEST ESCAPEES

In 1347 a Tartar army lay siege to the Italian colony of Caffa on the Black Sea of the Crimea. When the defenders turned back the attacks, the Tartars used catapults to shoot the bodies of their own dead soldiers over the walls into the city. The soldiers used as missiles had not died in battle. Some unknown disease had killed them.

When the Tartars finally took the city, a lucky few Italians escaped back to Italy, carrying with them the disease they'd caught from the Tartar missiles—the Black Death that spread throughout Europe and killed 20 million people.

UNLUCKY AT WORK

★ **Third Place:** The Surgeons
When a surgeon sews up a patient but leaves a scalpel inside by mistake, that's called "burying the hatchet."

★ **Runners-up:** The Pilots
Airline pilots refer to a midair collision as "swapping paint."

★ **And the Winners Are:** The Firefighters
When firefighters lose the battle and a building burns down to the ground, they call that "building a parking lot."

UNLUCKY IN GOLD

John Sutter had it made, raising cattle and sheep on a huge land-grant ranch in the Sacramento Valley of California. But a carpenter building a mill for Sutter got distracted by something shiny in the stream. What glittered was a few flakes of gold, which ruined everything Sutter had built by starting the gold rush of 1849.

Hundreds of miners dreaming of instant riches squatted on Sutter's land. He couldn't throw them off because there was no local law to back him up and his own men had all quit. No one wanted to work for wages anymore when they could go broke panning for gold.

Sutter went to the courts and then to Congress for help in getting rid of the 49ers. Even though he had clear legal title to the land and the miners had none, Sutter lost—his rights, his title, eventually his ranch. Private property, it turns out, was yours until it wasn't.

UNLUCKY IN SILVER

The Comstock Lode, once the richest silver mine in the world, did nothing for its founders, who went bust trying to mine it for gold in the 1800s.

Two brothers, Ethan and Hosea Grosh, opened the mine, but died before they could get any gold out of it. Henry Comstock, who took over the mine, also found no gold and sold it for next to nothing.

Then the professional miners moved in. They didn't find any gold either. But they did find a fortune in silver.

UNLUCKY IN THE LOTTERY

If some people weren't so lucky to begin with, they wouldn't be able to turn so unlucky.

In 2002 a West Virginia man won a $300 million lottery jackpot. Since then he's been burglarized twice, robbed once, and sued twice—once for assault and once for threatening assault.

But as the lottery people say: you can't be a winner if you're not a player.

UNLUCKY IN WORMS

Some fishermen use electric probes to draw earthworms to the surface so they can be turned into bait. Every now and then it's the fisherman who's turned into worm bait when he catches a bad jolt and electrocutes himself. Wormed to death.

UNLUCKY AT THIRTEENS

Composer Arnold Schoenberg had a dire superstition about the number thirteen and thought he would die on the thirteenth day of some month.

He did, dying on Friday, July 13, 1951, at thirteen minutes before midnight. He was seventy-six at the time (add the seven and the six to see where he ended up).

UNLUCKY AT THE COIN FLIP

Two Eskimo football teams had their game canceled in 1937 at King Island, Alaska, when a strong wind blew away their field, which was on an ice floe.

UNLUCKY AT THE PLATE

In 1935 Augie Galan of the Chicago Cubs went an entire season, with over six hundred at bats, without once hitting into a double play. What's so unlucky about that? He hit into a triple play.

UNLUCKY IN THE RING

A boxer named Jack Doyle, known as the Irish Thrush, missed a big roundhouse in the second round of his fight with Eddie Phillips. Although the force of Doyle's punch meant nothing to Phillips, it yanked Doyle over the ropes. He landed headfirst and knocked himself out.

UNLUCKY IN WAVES

Back in the sixties, the Beach Boys had a series of hit records that made surfing sound like too much fun. Kids who had never gone surfing before figured; How hard could surfing be if a bunch of doofs in plaid shorts can do it and still have time to learn to play the guitar, sort of?

Suddenly, Southern California beaches were packed with ordinary people who wanted to surf. This screwed it up for the get-there-first people who already were surfing (without the music), leading to unending surf wars between locals and anyone else who wanted to catch a wave.

UNLUCKY IN EMPIRE

Prior to the Roman Empire, the Roman army and everyone else had to slog over rough terrain. Rome built fifty thousand miles of

paved roads and used its fast-moving army to rule the slow people of the world.

Eventually, Rome's enemies realized that all roads lead to
Rome. The barbarians who encouraged the downfall of the Roman
Empire used Rome's own roads to get the job done.

UNLUCKY DOWN ON THE FARM

Farming in the fourteenth century was a brutal occupation—
long hours, few turnips, plenty of turnip thieves.

Then came the bubonic plague that killed a third of the people
in Europe, including a third of its farmers. Suddenly, there weren't
enough people left to work the land.

As an unintended consequence of the Black Death, the technology of farming was vastly improved so fewer people could do
more work. Unfortunately, that didn't help many of the farmers
since the bubonic plague had already buried them.

UNLUCKIEST LUNATICS

In Scotland for a thousand years, mad people were dunked in
the pool at Strathfillan, then bound with ropes and left in the
chapel of St. Fillian.

If the person freed himself by morning, he was considered
cured of his madness. This dubious medical practice was discon-
tinued in the enlightened nineteenth century when doctors found
more advanced methods—like shocking people with electricity—
to bring them to their senses.

UNLUCKY IN PETS

A man showed up at a New York City hospital one night claiming he had been bitten by a tiger in his apartment. When police went to the man's apartment, they found a four-hundred-pound tiger inside.

Why would a man keep a four-hundred-pound pet tiger inside an apartment in the middle of Manhattan?

What's it to you, pal? This is New York City, so forgeddaboutit.

UNLUCKIEST ROAD HOGS

They didn't drive cars, those first road hogs. In the 1890s road hogs referred to pushy bicycle riders who forced pedestrians to the side of the road. But it wasn't long before the pedestrians got cars and forced the bike riders off the road.

UNLUCKIEST LEADER

Horatio Nelson, the eighteenth century British admiral who defeated Napoleon's navy, was that rare leader who knows the difference between "Charge!" and "Follow me!"

Lucky in battle, Nelson had an incredible string of personal bad luck. Among other persistent illnesses during his command: malaria, rheumatism, and gout. Plus, he lost an arm in one battle and an eye in another.

One more problem that's really tough on a sailor: Admiral Nelson suffered from seasickness all the time he was at sea. Yet he soldiered on.

UNLUCKY IN POLITICS

That would be all of us, as economist John Kenneth Galbraith observed that "politics consists in choosing between the disastrous and the unpalatable."

UNLUCKY WINNERS

For over a hundred years the basic design of the bicycle has not changed. The rider still sits too high on an awkward seat pedaling into the wind.

Except for recumbent bikes (also known as human-powered vehicles). These redesigned bikes look like motorless cars, with the rider sitting down low. If you want to race them, add a plastic windshield that cuts down air resistance and an HPV can go twice as fast as an ordinary bike. Which is why they're never allowed in ordinary bike races. They're too fast.

Bicycle racing is one of those rare sports where world records are prevented from being broken by superior performers so as not to embarrass the other equipment manufacturers.

UNLUCKIEST GREEK GODS

1. Cronos.

Upside: boss god

Downside: bad diet, serious stomachaches, on the receiving end of a major case of pre-Oedipus oedipal complex

Being the first father, Cronos had no role models when it came to raising kids. So he swallowed them. This was the best idea the father of all the gods could come up with for protecting his throne from the kids.

For some reason, this didn't stop his wife Rhea from providing him with more kids for dinner.

But when Zeus came along, Rhea tricked her husband into swallowing a stone instead of the baby. This led to a bad case of indigestion, and Cronos vomited up his kids and the adopted stone.

But just because a Greek god is paranoid, it doesn't mean his kids don't want to banish him to the underworld. When Zeus grew up, he kicked his father out of his own kingdom. Rough family.

2. Hades.

The king of the underworld had dominion over the dead, guaranteeing him a never-ending supply of subjects, whereas his brother Zeus had to make them up as he went along.

For all his power and millions of minions, Hades couldn't get a date. "Nearly all-powerful god looking for queen. Vast underground kingdom can be yours. Plenty of servants. No sunbathing."

Things got so bad Hades had to ask his brother for permission to kidnap a bride. He got Persephone, not most gods' first choice. Hades found that out when he ran up against her mother Demeter, goddess of the harvest and the original mother-in-law from hell.

Demeter blackmailed Zeus. If she didn't get her daughter back, she would cancel all the Greek harvests, which meant a serious shortfall of offerings to the gods.

It looked like Hades would become the god of lonely old guys. But before Persephone could leave the underworld, he tricked her into eating seven seeds from one of his pomegranates. In the long tradition of trick fruit, those seeds condemned her for all eternity to spend seven months of the year in the underworld with Hades and only five months in the sunlight with Mom.

But as often happens, your worst enemies do you the biggest favors, inventing for Hades the perfect marriage. After seven months with the daughter of Demeter, Hades could enjoy a good stretch of peace and quiet. By the time Persephone came back to the underworld, she was probably looking pretty good.

Chapter 14

The Odd Hall of Fame

Normal people can become famous. Well, normality doesn't happen often. But fame alone is not enough to get you elected to the Odd Hall of Fame. You have to be famous and strange, like these winners:

MOST ARTISTIC JAILBIRD

French artist Maurice Utrillo was a notorious drunk, always in trouble with the law. Utrillo convinced Parisian gendarmes to keep brushes and paints in the jail so he could paint whenever he was locked up for the night.

THE GIRL LEAST LIKELY TO LIVE NEXT DOOR

Parker Posey starred in the offbeat films *The Doom Generation*, *Kicking and Screaming*, and *Party Girl*. In *The House of Yes* she played a crazy woman who thought she was Jackie Kennedy.

"She isn't the girl next door," her director for *The House of Yes* Mark Waters said about Parker, "unless you're living next door to the Addams Family."

MOST ARTISTIC FOOT

Surrealistic painter Salvador Dali sent someone else to buy his shoes because he refused to display his unshod feet in public.

MOST IRON-IC

The notorious John Wilkinson ran an eighteenth century English ironworks. He made a fortune crafting iron barrels for cannon.

Wilkinson liked working with iron so much that he invented iron money to pay his workers. He also built a church out of iron and gave iron coffins away as gifts.

MOST LIKELY TO LIKE CHIPMUNKS

Robert Ripley, who created the *Ripley's Believe It or Not* comic strip and museums, could have qualified for his own exhibits. When he drew his strips, he opened his office windows so chipmunks would run across his desk as he worked.

MOST LIKELY TO SCARE TURTLES

Artist Robert Rauschenberg staged a work of performance art in which thirty turtles were set loose on stage with flashlights strapped to their shells. Meanwhile, an actor danced with tin cans on his knees. Another actor ripped up a phone book. And three actresses walked through the auditorium in bridal gowns handing out crackers to the audience. Now why didn't I think of that?

MOST LIKELY NOT TO ROCK

Tim Raines was a terrific hitter for the Montreal Expos. When he signed with the Chicago White Sox in 1991, Tim decided to change his name to Rock Raines. His .300 batting average dropped like a rock, to .106.

Rock went back to calling himself Tim, and his batting average immediately righted itself.

LEAST LIKELY TO CHANGE CLOTHES

When San Francisco Giants shortstop Johnnie LeMaster was struggling at the plate, the fans turned on him. So he tried to change the name on the back of his uniform from Lemaster to Boo. But management, being neither as strange nor as funny as stars, wouldn't go along with the idea.

ODD TALENT RIBBONS

You can be odd without having exceptional talents. Or you can be talented without being odd, although that doesn't happen often. These ribbons are awarded to people who, if they didn't have odd enough talents, worked harder until they did.

THE ADAM AND EVE MEMORIAL DISAPPEARING FIG LEAF: RECOGNIZING TALENTED INNOVATIONS IN NUDITY

★ **Third Place:** The Painter

French painter Amedeo Modigliani took to stripping off all his clothes in Parisian bistros and reciting poetry naked.

"Look at me," he would shout to a café full of tourists, "beautiful as a newborn babe, or just out of the bath. Don't I look like a god?"

★ **Runner-up:** The President

When Theodore Roosevelt was president, he liked to swim naked in the middle of winter to get the day started—and pressured lobbyists and other politicians into joining him.

★ **And the Winners Are:** The Prankster Brothers

On-screen comics Groucho and Harpo Marx were offscreen jokers. Going to a bachelor party, the movie stars decided to surprise their friend by emerging from the hotel elevator naked, wearing nothing but their top hats.

But they pressed the button for the wrong floor and emerged into a party being thrown for the bride-to-be. The marriage went ahead the next day anyway.

THE DESPERATE HOBBY ASSOCIATION AWARD:
PROVING THAT EVERYBODY NEEDS A HOBBY AND EVERY CONCEIVABLE HOBBY NEEDS A PERSON

★ **Third Place:** Predator Calling

In this Western competition, contestants try to convince a coyote, bobcat, or fox to target them as food by imitating the calls of dying rabbits or rodents.

★ **Runner-up:** Bottle Cap Collecting

Most people toss them away, but the owners of Miami's Bottle Cap Inn covered the walls with three hundred thousand bottle caps in 1939.

★ **And the Winner Is:** Card Spotting

Some people look for coins on the street. Frank Damek had an eye for spotting lost playing cards on the streets of Chicago. Took him thirty years to complete a full deck of found cards, but he did it.

THE WONDER IF I CAN DO THAT PRIZE:
FOR ODD TALENTS PEOPLE GET REALLY GOOD AT ALTHOUGH NO ONE ELSE CAN FIGURE OUT WHY

★ **Third Place:** The Plowman

Albrecht Ringling, founder of one of the nation's great circuses, also had his own act: he would balance a farm plow on his chin.

★ **Runner-up:** The Climber

In 1977 Emma Disley climbed the tallest mountain in Wales. It was only four thousand feet, not a major climbing feat—except that she did it on stilts.

★ **And the Winner Is:** The Swimmer

Johnny Pearce from North Carolina swam two and a half miles one day in 1930. Nothing remarkable about that, except that he swam it smoking a pipe all the way.

THE ROCKY COW–SPARRING TROPHY:
GIVEN TO SUPERSTAR ATHLETES WITH UNUSUAL TRAINING REGIMENS

★ **Third Place:** The Rocker

The great pitcher Grover Cleveland Alexander was born to a large Nebraska farm family. He developed his remarkable accuracy early and without the aid of a baseball.

When his mother sent him out to the chicken yard to get the family a bird for dinner, Grover would bring it down with a rock. When he went hunting, he didn't need a rifle. He brought down game armed only with rocks.

★ **Runner-up:** The Runner

On a train ride across country to compete in the Los Angeles Olympics of 1928, Babe Didrikson kept in shape by jogging the length of the train, car by car, forward and back.

★ **And the Winners Are:** The Pitchers

A tie between two of the greatest pitchers in baseball history, Roger Clemens and Nolan Ryan.

Clemens borrowed a technique from karate black belts: he strengthened his fingers by exercising them in bowls of uncooked rice. Ryan toughened his pitching hand by soaking it in pickle brine.

MAD MONEY AWARDS: FOR PEOPLE WHO FIND UNUSUAL ALTERNATIVES TO COLD HARD CASH

★ **Third Place:** The Dental Check

The painter Marcel Duchamp offered to pay his dentist with a drawing of a check, which listed the bank as the Teeth's Loan and Trust Company.

The dentist was happy to accept such an unusual payment. He sold the drawing for far more than the dental work was worth.

★ **Runner-up:** The Nail Exchange

In 1767 Captain Samuel Wallis landed his ship in Tahiti, the first European to set foot on the island. His sailors spent their time with native girls. The price of their recreation? Iron nails, which they pulled from the planks of the ship. They were lucky the ship held together long enough for them to sail away again.

★ **And the Winner Is:** Big Bananas

An El Paso electronics store named Silo advertised a stereo set for the "low price of 299 bananas" in 1985.

The store's flip ad backfired when hundreds of customers showed up toting bags of bananas—the yellow, fruity kind—demanding their deal. The store had to live up to its promise, and the owners ate the loss.

THE SALT OR GOLD TROPHY, YOUR CHOICE: GOES TO A TIE BETWEEN GOLD AND SALT

Salt is so common that restaurants give it away. They rarely give away gold. But salt was once worth its weight in gold.

In the Dark and Middle Ages merchants from Arab and European lands risked dangerous journeys into sub-Saharan Africa to trade for gold. The natives there had ample gold, which they considered worthless, except that these strange outsiders would give them salt for it.

Since these Africans had no salt mines of their own, gold was worth its weight in salt. Don't you wish you could still make that deal?

The trading system was as unusual as the deal itself. The merchant traders would leave the salt on the ground, then return to their ship or caravan and send up a smoke signal. The African gold miners would take the salt, leave the gold, and fade back into the jungle. Then the traders would return for their reward.

Neither of the bartering parties ever met. But each party was certain it had snookered the other—trading something of little value for something of great value.

THE GIFT-WRAPPED TROPHY:
FOR ORIGINALITY IN GIFT GIVING

★ **Third Place:** The Perfect Stone

When playwright George Bernard Shaw visited the Holy Land in 1931, he brought back for a friend an unusual souvenir—a small stone he had plucked from the road in Bethlehem.

Why bring a pebble back to England? "Who knows," Shaw explained, "whose footprints may be on the stone?"

★ **Runner-up:** The Thought that Counts

Movie director Alfred Hitchcock was rumored to be infatuated with actress Tippi Hedren when she starred in his film, *The Birds*.

When Tippi's daughter, Melanie Griffith, celebrated her sixth birthday, the eccentric filmmaker gave the girl a tiny coffin containing a wax replica of her mother.

★ **And the Winner Is:** The Grab Bag

Cal Suggs made a fortune running a Texas cattle ranch. Late in life he gave much of his money away.

To the girl graduating with top grades from a San Angelo high school each year, the millionaire offered a choice of three prizes. She could have a diamond, a car, or a year's scholarship to college.

Suggs then gave a young friend this advice about choosing a wife: "Pick only the one who chooses the scholarship."

THE ORIGINAL SALES PROMOTION PRIZE GOES TO HUNTINGTON BEACH

Land in Southern California was once considered so worthless that sections of Huntington Beach were given away to anyone who bought an encyclopedia.

When oil was discovered there, it made the people who'd gone for the book deal rich.

THE DEVOLUTION AWARDS: FOR PEOPLE WHO BEHAVE LIKE ANIMALS

★ **Third Place:** The Monkeys

To rehearse for *Quest for Fire*, Hollywood's most realistic film about prehistoric life, director Jean-Jacques Annaud put his actors through three months of training in simian behavior.

"We spent much time on all fours like chimps," star Everett McGill said. "And it worked. When shooting began, we had all that residual behavior stored up."

★ **Runner-up:** The Donkeys

Throughout Europe in the Middle Ages, people celebrated December 28 as the Feast of Fools. When priests held mass on this day, the congregation would respond by braying like donkeys.

★ **And the Winner Is:** The Fox

The spread of suburban housing developments throughout England has threatened the pursuit of the fox by England's upper class. One alternative: the fox hunters have gotten rid of the fox, which tends to run wherever it pleases to get away from the hounds—including into people's backyards—and substituted joggers.

Bloodhounds follow the trail of these human foxes, and hunters on horseback follow the dogs. Great sport, what?

WINNERS OF THE CELEBRITY ANIMAL WANNA-BE CONTEST

★ **Third Place:** Writer William Faulkner

Thinking about reincarnation, the novelist mused, "I'd want to come back a buzzard. Nothing hates him or envies him or wants him or needs him. He is never bothered or in danger, and he can eat anything."

★ **Runner-up:** Movie Star Richard Gere

"I know who I am," the movie star declared in 2002. "No one else knows who I am. If I was a giraffe and somebody said I was a snake, I'd think 'No, actually I am a giraffe.'"

★ **And the Winner Is:** Playwright Eugene O'Neill

"It was a great mistake my being born a man," O'Neill once said.

Did the author of some of America's greatest tragedies really want to be a woman? No.

"I would have been more successful as a seagull or a fish," he explained.

Chapter 15

The Un-Oscars:
Prince Cheeseburger and
Other Award-Winning Fakes

The urge to imitate is a creative impulse. As painter Salvador Dali pointed out, "Those who do not want to imitate anything, produce nothing."

Those who willingly imitate produce, among other things, television and pop music.

The Oscars always go to actors who are given everything: scripts, directors, stunt men. These Un-Oscars go to stars who also pretend to be what they're not. But working without scripts, directors, or a Hollywood budget, they have to make it up as they go along.

Best Madonna

In 2003 a woman vacationing in Hawaii volunteered to be part of a stage act. She was hypnotized and told to act like Madonna.

The woman jumped down from the stage and attacked the resort's security guards.

Best Mega-Elvis

Elvis, is there no end in sight? Nope, none. On what would have been the King's sixty-eighth birthday in 2003, two teams of Elvis impersonators played a basketball game during the halftime of a non-Elvis NBA game between the Chicago Bulls and Utah Jazz.

Best Actors in a Nonsupporting Role

In eighteenth-century England when patients were released from the madhouse, they were given a government license to beg for food. These Bedlamites were often outbegged by other poor people with forged licenses who pretended to be mad so they could cash in on the deal.

Best Baldies

The Seattle Mariners threw a Jay Buhner Buzz Cut Night in honor of their popular slugger in 1996, giving away free tickets before the game to everyone who agreed to have their hair shaved off on the field.

How many hair-free people took the team up on its offer? Including 28 women, 3,321.

Best No-Name Star

Walter Cronkite started out in radio as Walter Wilcox. Why? Because radio stations at the time were worried that newsmen would become popular with listeners, then go to work for another station and take the listeners with them.

Station managers reasoned that if they made up names for their announcers, the newsmen could leave but the names would belong to the station. Then the station could simply call the next announcer by the same name, and the listeners wouldn't know the difference.

When Walter Wilcox quit his first Kansas City radio station, he had to revert to being Walter Cronkite, under which name he became the most famous anchor in TV history.

Best Wasp

The English hover fly is a method actor, playing the part of a tough guy even though he's a softie at heart. This biteless fly protects itself by pretending to be a wasp. To convince birds, the fly imitates the way a wasp buzzes. Birds, wary of getting stung, avoid the fly even though it has no stinger.

Best Five-Legged Wasp Stand-in

Among cross-dressing wasp impersonators, the South American cricket believes in flying softly and carrying a fake stick.

This six-legged cricket looks waspish and uses one of its legs as a fake stinger. The cricket points the fake stinger at predators and walks on five legs to trick them into keeping their distance.

Best Fake Set Design

Tourists flock to the beautiful sands of Waikiki Beach, but it's only pretending to be a beach. All the sand was imported from other beaches because Waikiki was originally a swamp.

Best Stand-in

A wolf killed the seeing-eye dog of the blind St. Harvey of Wales. The wolf felt so bad about what he'd done that he agreed to serve the saint in the dog's place.

Best Caterer

When St. Giles of France lived as a hermit in a cave, a deer brought him milk each day so he wouldn't starve.

Best Double

Pop artist Andy Warhol painted canvases of soup can labels that looked exactly like the real thing and portraits of famous people that looked like their photos.

When he agreed to go on a college lecture tour, he sent a friend instead, who pretended to be Andy Warhol.

Best Actors

"Most people are other people," the Irish playwright Oscar Wilde pointed out. "Their thoughts are someone else's opinions. Their lives a mimicry. Their passions a quotation."

Best Props

Wedgwood china is now a collector's item. But when English potter Josiah Wedgwood first made it, his work was an imitation of Delft porcelain from Holland, which was an imitation of Chinese china, which was too expensive for most collectors or anyone who wanted something to eat dinner of.

Best Musical Score

Queen Victoria praised composer Felix Mendelssohn's "Songs Without Words." Then the composer admitted that he hadn't written them. His sister, Fanny Hensel, had.

Mendelssohn had taken the credit because he didn't think a woman could be successful as a composer.

Best Art Direction

Before he created the vastly successful comic strip *Peanuts*, Charles Schulz taught himself to draw by copying the comic book spaceman Buck Rogers, Popeye, and the Disney cartoons.

THE DOUBLE-TAKE PRIZES: HONORING WINNERS THAT ARE NOT WHAT THEY APPEAR TO BE

The Galaxy of Contradictions Trophy: For conclusions that would be obvious except for the fact that they're false

★ **Third Place:** The Big Dipper

In North America, the Big Dipper remains one of our favorite constellations, except for the annoyingly persistent fact that it's not actually a constellation. It's only part of Ursa Major. Now that's a constellation.

★ **Runner-up:** Stars

Stars don't twinkle. They only look like they do when viewed from Earth. It's the air moving around our sky that makes the light from stars flicker. From space, stars shine with a steady, untwinkling light.

★ **And the Winner Is:** Shoes

Seven out of ten Americans who own running shoes don't use them to run.

THE TRUTH IS NOT ONLY STRANGER THAN FICTION BUT RARER TOO AWARD

★ **Third Place:** The Next to the Last Mohican

James Fenimore Cooper immortalized the wildness of the American wilderness and the courage of the men who tamed the frontier in the early 1800s through books like *The Last of the Mohicans*, *The Deerslayer*, and *The Pathfinder*.

Cooper, unlike his invincible woodsman hero Natty Bumpo, had never been near the wilderness. He was a gentleman farmer who lived in the safety and comfort of an upstate New York home while his imagination roamed.

★ **Runner-up:** The East Virginian

The tough, stalwart image of the Old West cowboy was promoted by author Owen Wister, who wrote *The Virginian*. But Wister was not a man of the saddle. He was an intellectual Easterner.

★ **And the Winner Is:** The Cowboy Hat

Cowboys in the Old West didn't call their cowboy hats "cowboy hats." That was an Eastern fancy, picked up and promoted by dime novelists.

Cowboys called their hats "hats," sensibly enough. They wore the big hats with wide brims for another sensible reason—out on the open range, it was the only protection they had against the baking sun and pounding rain.

That famous Stetson hat? Not the vision of a larger-than-life Texan, but an East Coast invention. John B. Stetson wasn't a cowboy. He was a Philly hatmaker of the 1860s with a vision of big profits.

THE SCUBA CLIMBERS TROPHY: GOES TO PEOPLE WHO CLIMB MOUNTAINS BECAUSE PART OF IT WAS THERE

Edmund Hillary and Tenzing Norgay were the first two mountain climbers to not quite climb the world's tallest mountain.

First, there were probably other climbers who made it to the top of Mount Everest before Hillary and Norgay did it in 1953. But they didn't make it all the way back down again.

Second, Mount Everest isn't the tallest mountain in the world. That would be Mauna Kea in Hawaii (measured from its undersea base), at 33,476 feet, which is 4,441 feet taller than Mount Everest.

Mauna Kea gets slighted because two thirds of the island's mountain is under the ocean. But why should that challenge stop mountain climbers?

THE PRIMITIVE PRIZE: FOR HISTORIC ADVANCES THAT MAKE CIVILIZED PEOPLE LOOK EXACTLY LIKE THEIR PRIMITIVE ANCESTORS

★ **Third Place:** Football

The gridiron game dates back to the third century when young men from two English villages would fight over an animal's bladder, the closest thing they had to a ball.

Each side tried to move the bladder back to the other side's village. Beating your opponents till they couldn't stand was considered an effective strategy for moving the bladder.

This game eventually led to soccer, rugby, and American football—a game we often view as preparing men for the battles of life. But the English saw the game producing the opposite result.

Many men were badly injured during these games—rendering them unfit to go kill each other in battle. So the game was banned by English kings from 1314 to 1603.

★ **Runner-up:** Gold

People are most attached not to reality but to illusion. Through the ages man has pursued the most illusionary of riches: gold. Ignoring the historic evidence, men convince themselves they can find it and then hold on to it.

Gold is valued for its indestructibility, whereas the owner remains easily destroyed because of the gold. As soon as he gets it, other illusion seekers will take it away from him.

★ **And the Winner Is:** Money

On the islands of Yap in Micronesia, money was historically kept in the form of large round stones. The larger the stone, the more it was worth.

Eventually, the stones became too large to carry or even lift to hand over as portable currency. So when money was exchanged, the stone was left where it lay. Title alone was transferred.

This system sounded comical to Westerners when they first encountered it. Actually, it foreshadowed the industrial world's conversion to electronic banking, where cyber-money is transferred from owner to owner while the gold (should there actually be any) stays in the vault.

THE LIFE'S A DRAG PRIZE:
RECOGNIZING ACHIEVEMENTS IN OTHER PEOPLE'S CLOTHES

★ **Third Place:** The Lady in the Tux

Movie vamp Marlene Dietrich liked to pose for publicity stills in a tuxedo like one of the boys, with her male costars (like Gary Cooper and Maurice Chevalier) flanking her also wearing tuxedos.

Rival screen star Louise Brooks said of Dietrich and her penchant for cross-dressing, "It's like Oscar Wilde said, that nothing looks so innocent as an indiscretion."

★ **Runner-up:** Great Gatsby!

Writer F. Scott Fitzgerald became a figure as romantic as any of his books, notorious for his wild love affairs and dissolute marriage to Zelda. But in college, Fitzgerald amused himself by putting on a dress and going to university dances with a male friend. He also acted in drag for college shows.

★ **And the Winner Is:** The King's a Queen

In the 1600s Christina, the daughter of King Gustavus Adolphus, ascended to the throne of Sweden. But she did not become a queen.

Instead, she was crowned King Christina. By Swedish custom, only a king's wife could be called a queen.

THE TRAVEL IS NOT SO BROADENING PRIZE: GOES TO OHIO

If you've traveled from Dublin to London, then on to Geneva, Moscow, Berlin, Holland, Poland, Cadiz, Lisbon, Antwerp, New Paris, and New Vienna—then you've never left Ohio.

Many immigrant groups settled in that cosmopolitan state, then named their towns after the places they'd come from.

THE BARGAIN OF THE CENTURY PRIZE

In 1925 two Duluth men chipped in and bought their town its own NFL franchise. How much did they pay to join what would become the nation's most popular and profitable sport? $1.00. They should have bought two.

THE BE ALL YOU CAN BE . . . SOMEWHERE ELSE MEDAL

Michael Jordan didn't make his high school basketball team. Plenty of other award winners looked like they'd never make it early in their careers.

★ **Third Place:** They Also Serve Who Only Get Out of the Way

Some people help to build a better army by going into some other line of work.

The poet of the macabre, Edgar Allan Poe, went to West Point but was allowed to resign after studiously ignoring his military studies.

Marcel Proust graduated fifty-ninth out of a class of sixty cadets from military college—but did better as a writer.

Other writers who spent time in military schools: the poet Ezra Pound, Truman Capote (*In Cold Blood*), Edgar Rice Burroughs (Tarzan) and L. Frank Baum (*The Wizard of Oz*).

★ **Runner-up:** 250 Losers

Jockey Eddie Arcaro won 4,779 races in his career. But when he started riding, he lost 250 races in a row.

★ **And the Winner Is:** The Nonquitter

Orel Hershiser, one of baseball's best pitchers, was cut from his high school baseball team in his freshman year. He was cut again in his sophomore year.

In college Hershiser managed to duplicate this feat (most players would have quit trying by then) when he was cut from the baseball team in both freshman and sophomore years.

Finally, he made a team—the Dodgers, where he became one of the best pitchers of his generation.

THE STAR SEARCH PRIZE:
BECAUSE TODAY'S LOSERS ARE TOMORROW'S STARS

★ **Third Place:** Or Second Place, as They Call It in San Francisco

Before he became famous, Robin Williams entered the San Francisco Stand-up Comedy Competition and came in second.

★ **Runner-up:** So-So in Ho-Ho

In high school Woody Allen's classmates voted him second for Class Comedian.

★ **And the Winner Is:** The Loser

At the age of nine, Christina Aguilera sang on the American TV talent show *Star Search*. She lost.

Great Moments in Social Confusion, as the United States Takes on the World

It's a small, small confusing world, and the ways we do things here may be the opposite of the way they do them over there.

1. In the U.S.A. nodding your head up and down means you agree with someone.

But in India, it means you disagree. Shaking your head from side to side, that means yes, although it means no in the U.S.A.

2. In the United States the guest of honor is usually seated next to or near the host at a dinner party.

In China the guest of honor sits opposite the host, with other important people flanking the guest. Following this system, those lowest in social rank end up sitting next to the host.

3. In the United States romantic couples may hold hands walking down the street or put their arms around each other in public. But friends of the same sex don't do that, except in San Francisco.

In Indonesia men and women have no contact in public, no kissing, hugging, or handholding. But friends of the same sex often hold hands in public or walk with their arms around each other. This does not mean they are homosexual, as it implies in America.

4. In U.S. business when people say, "Let me think about it," they mean they haven't decided yet.

In Japan "Let me think about it" is a polite way of saying "no" without having to say no.

5. In the United States not finishing a meal when you're a guest in someone's home slights your host.

But in China finishing all the food on your plate is insulting because it implies that your host did not give you enough to eat.

6. In Belgium it's considered rude if you talk to someone with your hands in your pockets.

In the United States it's only rude if you have your hands in *their* pockets.

7. In England if you want to be called sir, you have to pay the queen for the privilege.

In the United States all you have to do is go down to the local Burger King and they'll call you sir every time.

England has its royalty, but we have a Burger King and a Dairy Queen. If they ever get married, they might produce America's own royalty, Prince Cheeseburger.

Chapter 16

Best of the Quick and the Slow

We all know about the people who march to the beat of a different drummer. But what about the folks who mambo to the beat of a really different drummer? They win the Sit Down Band Awards for the Quick and the Slow.

THE SLOW DOWN, YOU MOVE TOO FAST PRIZES

THE TENTH PLACE TROPHY: GOES TO THE DRIVER WHO CAN'T LOSE

During the 1912 Indy 500, race car driver Ralph Mulford found himself alone on the track after nine cars had crossed the finish line and the rest of the pack dropped out of the race with mechanical problems.

Knowing he would finish tenth and pick up some prize money, Mulford stopped for dinner, then took eight hours and fifty-three minutes to finish the race.

THE SLOW PAINT PRIZE

Dutch painter Jan Vermeer was considered a master. But he painted so slowly that when he died he left his wife with eleven children and no money. She had to trade two of his paintings to the town baker for bread.

THE SLOW RIDE PRIZE

When the first elevators were installed in Manhattan office buildings in 1879, the cars rose so slowly they were built with benches so passengers could sit during their long vertical journeys.

THE LAZY DREAMER PRIZE

Car manufacturer Henry Ford confounded an efficiency expert who complained about one of Ford's workers, a man who spent much of the workday sitting in his office with his feet up on his desk daydreaming.

"He's wasting your money," the consultant pointed out to the tycoon.

Ford explained that the man had once devised an idea that saved the company millions. "And at the time his feet were planted right where they are now," Ford said.

THE LONG CONCLUSION PRIZE

After developing the theory of evolution as a young scientist, Charles Darwin took twenty years to figure out the details and publish his ideas in *On the Origin of Species*.

THE SLOW NOBEL PRIZE

When he was thirty-one, biologist Francis Rous studied chicken viruses. Fifty-five years later he was awarded the Nobel Prize for his work.

THE SLOW FAME PRIZE

While success is often achieved by Type A people who push harder to become Type A+ people, others believe in the maxim: never put off till tomorrow what you can put off till next Thursday.

★ **Third Place:** The Clerk
At nineteen George Bernard Shaw quit his job as an office clerk and lived off his mother while trying to become a writer. He had no real success for seventeen years
Finally, at thirty-six he had his first play produced and went on to become one of the most successful playwrights of the Western world.

★ **Runner-up:** The Slow Writer
Historian Edward Gibbon took twenty-three years to write his six-volume masterpiece, *The History of the Decline and Fall of the Roman Empire*.

★ **And the Winner Is:** The Banker

Painter Paul Cezanne worked his entire career as a banker. In his off-hours, he painted for thirty-four years before he had his first one-man show at the age of fifty-six. Now he's recognized as one of the world's great painters.

THE GOING NOWHERE SLOWLY PRIZE

During the Civil War, a businessman asked President Lincoln for a pass so he could travel to Richmond, capital of the Confederacy.

Lincoln responded, "Within the last two years, I have given passes to 250,000 men to go to Richmond, and not one has got there yet."

THE TIMING IS EVERYTHING AWARD

Speed thrills, but to the slow belongs the sly amusements of the caustic wit.

★ **Third Place:** Evelyn Waugh

The British writer nailed it when he said, "Punctuality is the virtue of the bored."

★ **Runner-up:** Mark Twain

"Never put off until tomorrow what you can do the day after tomorrow," the author of *Huckleberry Finn* advised us.

★ **And the Winner Is:** Jules Renard

"Laziness is nothing more than the habit of resting before you get tired," the French writer said.

THE LAST SLOW WORD PRIZE:
GOES TO RADIO WIT OSCAR LEVANT

"So little time." Oscar sighed. "So little to do."

THE ARE YOU DONE YET?
QUICK-THINKING AWARDS

THE FAST PROFIT TROPHIES:
FOR ORIGINALITY IN MONEYMAKING

★ **Third Place:** Silver City

When turn-of-the-century floods cut through Silver City, New Mexico, the water turned Main Street into a fifty-five-foot-deep arroyo.

Didn't faze Main Street shop owners, though. They simply cut doors into the backs of their shops, turning the backs into the fronts, and Bullard Street became the new main street of the town.

★ **Runner-up:** The Collection Man

Wealthy merchant Julius Rosenwald had an original method of collecting money from debtors. He sent them a note explaining that if they did not pay their bill immediately, "we shall be obliged to notify your other creditors that you paid us." That brought in the money quickly enough.

★ **And the Winner Is:** The Bearded Wonder

Georges de Saint-Foix was a French poet often in debt, but never lacking in clever ways to get by. One merchant to whom he owed much money followed Saint-Foix into a barbershop, where the poet was settling in for a shave.

When the creditor demanded money, Saint-Foix politely asked if the merchant would wait until he was shaved. When the merchant agreed to the request, the poet rose from the barber chair and left. He proceeded to grow a beard that he wore for the rest of his life.

THE SNAPPY COMEBACK SOCIETY'S COACH'S QUIP OF THE YEAR AWARD

★ **Third Place:** Football Coach Duffy Daugherty

The Michigan State coach put the game in perspective when he told reporters, "When you're playing for the national championship, it's not a matter of life and death. It's more important than that."

★ **Runner-up:** Baseball Manager Casey Stengel

The Old Professor found a way to straighten out slugger Mickey Mantle early in his career. When Mantle was a rookie with the New York Yankees, pitchers found him easy enough to strike out. Embarrassed after yet another whiff, Mantle battered the dugout watercooler with a bat.

Finally, the veteran manager got through to the rookie. "Son," Casey explained, "it ain't the watercooler that's striking you out."

★ **And the Winner Is:** Football Coach Jeff Cravath

After Cravath quit coaching at USC, he started a cattle ranch, which he liked better than college football because "cattle don't have any alumni."

THE QUICK SHOT TROPHY:
FOR HEROES WHO OUTTHINK THE ENEMY

★ **Third Place:** Any One Soldier

During World War I, a British official asked the French military leader Ferdinand Foch what was the minimum number of British troops he would need sent over the Channel to help win the war.

Foch replied that the British only needed to send him one soldier.

"I will see that he is killed at once," Foch explained. "Then the whole British Empire will come to avenge him."

★ **Runner-up:** The Defensive Rumor

During the Civil War, the Drayton Hall plantation in Charleston, South Carolina, was saved from being torched by Union soldiers when the owners spread a rumor that their house was being used to treat smallpox victims.

★ **And the Winner Is:** Strategic Lighting

British warships attacked the town of St. Michaels, Maryland, at night during the War of 1812. The sailors aimed their cannons at the town lights and blasted them into darkness. Then the ships sailed on.

What the British navy didn't know was that the people of St. Michaels had hung lanterns high in the trees, then darkened their houses. When the British fleet attacked in the dark, the ships hit only the tops of the trees. The town was spared.

THE CLOCK WATCHERS TROPHY:
FOR RAPID REFINEMENTS IN TIME MANAGEMENT

★ **Third Place:** Seventeen Minutes

When movie mogul Louis B. Mayer went to meet Franklin Roosevelt in the White House, the producer put his watch on the president's desk, explaining that he'd been told if anyone "spends eighteen minutes with you, you have them."

Mayer listened to the president for seventeen minutes, then left.

★ Runner-up: Fifteen Minutes

Movie star Mae West had an efficient style of writing her scripts that would impress productivity experts everywhere.

"One time I got a whole picture, 'Every Day's a Holiday'; it came to me in fifty-six seconds," she recalled. "It took me fifteen minutes to tell it to my producer and director, and another forty-five minutes to dictate it to a typist. It was one of my best pictures."

★ And the Winner Is: Minute One

Chinese Emperor Shih Huang Ti ordered his soldiers to gather all the books in his realm and burn them in 212 B.C. Why? He felt he was such a magnificent emperor that history should start all over again, counting from the Year of Him.

THE QUICK AND THE MARRIED AWARDS: FOR QUICK THINKING AT THE ALTAR

★ Third Place: A Good Reason to Object

St. Uncumber of Portugal didn't want to marry as her father the king commanded. So she made herself unweddable by growing a beard and mustache overnight.

★ Runner-up: A Good Reason to Marry Slowly

A century ago Alabamans preferred long wedding ceremonies. A state custom maintained that whoever rose first from the altar, husband or wife, would be the first to die.

★ **And the Winner Is:** A Good Reason to Say I Do

In Arkansas in the 1800s, a married man could decline a challenge to a duel from a bachelor under the theory that an unmarried man didn't risk equal responsibility in the duel.

THE UNITED CHAD HANGERS PRIZE:
FOR FAST-THINKING IN POLITICS

★ **Third Place:** Mayor for a Day

When John Lindsay was elected mayor of New York City in 1965, he immediately ran into two big problems: a citywide blackout and a transit strike on his first day in office.

Or as the newspaper writer Dick Schaap put it: "Only one day in office and he has already eliminated crime in the subway."

★ **Runner-up:** Republican for a Minute

Theodore Roosevelt was interrupted during a campaign speech by a heckler who shouted that he'd never vote for a Republican because he had always been a Democrat, his father had been a Democrat, and his grandfather had been a Democrat."

"Suppose your grandfather had been a jackass and your father was a jackass," Roosevelt countered. "What would you then be?"

"A Republican," the heckler replied.

★ **And the Winner Is:** The Water Test

When John McClellan of Arkansas ran for reelection to the Senate, he engaged his opponent in dueling speeches at a county fair.

The challenger went first and gave his stump speech, then paused to pour a glass of water from a pitcher on the stage. But while posing for a news photo, he missed the glass and poured the water over the heads of some people standing in front of the stage.

McClellan dropped his own stump speech on the spot. He took the stage and asked the crowd one question: "Do you want a senator who's too dumb to pour water into a glass?"

THE QUICK DRAW ARTISTS' PRIZE: FOR INSTANT ART

★ **Third Place:** On the Road

Beat writer Jack Kerouac wrote his breakthrough novel *On the Road* in only three weeks. It then took him six years to get the book published. It turned out to be a best seller.

★ **Runner-up:** On His Head

When Robin Williams auditioned for the role of Mork from Ork in the TV show that proved to be his breakthrough to the big time, director Garry Marshall pointed to a chair and told him to sit down. Robin did sit, but upside down on his head.

Marshall gave him the extraterrestrial role on the spot, saying he was the only alien who had shown up for the audition.

★ **And the Winner Is:** On the Clock

Before French writer Georges Simenon started on a novel, he would go to the doctor for a complete physical. Then he would lock himself in his rooms and give himself seven days to write the book and three days to edit it. He wrote more than five-hundred books this way.

QUICKEST WEATHER REPORT

In the mountains of the South, they say you can predict the weather for the year based on the weather you get during the first twelve days of January. For example, if you have good weather on January 9 that means September will be a good month.

Chapter 17

The Foodie Cups:
Worm Soda and Other
Award-Winning Recipes

"I want my food dead," comic Woody Allen explained, refusing to eat oysters, "not sick, not wounded—dead."

That's the great thing about food. When there's enough to go around, it's to each their own. But when it comes to Foodie Awards, you've got to have really odd taste to win.

THE NOT THAT HUNGRY TROPHY:
FOR FOOD IDEAS THAT TEST THIS THEORY—NO MATTER
HOW GROSS IT SOUNDS, IT'S SOMEBODY'S DISH

★ **Third Place:** Pass the Vaseline
In India Vaseline is popular as a spread on bread.

★ **Runner-up:** Pass the Bucket

To attract diners on the Atkins and other antibread diets, a pizzeria in Escondido, California, came up with the perfect non-pizza pizza.

Pizza-in-a-Bucket has everything that goes on top of the pizza but nothing that goes below the topping.

Doughless pizza should fit neatly with spaghetti and meatballs without the spaghetti, PB&J without the bread, or crackerless cheese and crackers.

★ **And the Winner Is:** Pass the Worms

In the 1950s a soda maker in Wisconsin put out a soft drink called Worm Soda. Who could resist the promise of opening "a can of worms"?

THE FAKE FOOD TROPHY: GOES TO THE U.S. ARMY, LEGUME BRIGADE

In the 1970s the army conducted tests to change the mess menu, based on which foods the soldiers liked and what they couldn't stomach.

When they asked soldiers to rank their food preferences, the army pollsters included on the list a fake food they called funistrada.

Although the GIs had never eaten something that didn't exist, soldiers still voted funistrada better than lima beans.

THE BUTTER BATTLE PRIZE:
FOR MILESTONES IN THE WAR BETWEEN
BUTTER AND MARGARINE

★ **Third Place:** License to Oleo

In 1902 it was called a dangerous drug. Stores needed a license before they could sell it to the public. That dangerous drug would be margarine, of course.

★ **Runner-up:** Separate but Equal

In Germany at the turn of the twentieth century, if you wanted to buy margarine instead of butter, you had to enter the grocery store through a separate but equal door.

★ **And the Winner Is:** I Can't Believe It's Not Pink Butter

In the early 1900s, margarine threatened the dairy industry's kitchen monopoly. The dairy industry fought back by influencing legislators to pass laws that margarine manufacturers had to dye their product pink so consumers wouldn't be fooled into thinking it was butter.

Ironically, food coloring was often added to butter to fool the public into thinking it was more golden than nature could manage on her own.

GREAT MOMENTS IN THE KITCHEN

1. Salt is edible dirt.

2. Instant pudding has more salt in it than potato chips.

3. Americans are putting on too much weight? Duh! Can't count this medical release as a big surprise since the average American eats eighteen pounds of candy and drinks thirty-six gallons of soda each year.

4. In 1929 7-Up was sold to hospitals as a hangover cure. At the same time, people used it as a mixer for drinks that caused hangovers.

5. When ice cream was popularized in the mid-1800s, health officials warned consumers that ice cream lowered the body's temperature, interfering with digestion. Their medical advice? Never eat ice cream after a meal.

6. When malted milk was created in the 1880s, it was sold as a health food for babies.

7. Hershey's Kisses got their name because the machine that makes them looks like it's kissing the conveyor belt. Just think— there are machines out there more romantic than you are.

8. In 1987 American Airlines saved $40,000 by eliminating one olive from each first-class salad.

Didn't work for me. I eliminated one olive from my salad and saved nothing except that jar of olives in the fridge for another year.

THE ORIGINAL RECIPE AWARD: FOR COMMON FOODS WE PROBABLY WOULDN'T EAT TODAY IF THEY STILL MADE THEM THE WAY THEY USED TO

★ **Third Place:** The Horseradish Substitute

Heinz, the ketchup people, started out making horseradish, which they put in clear bottles because the competition put theirs in colored bottles.

Why did scurrilous food manufacturers use colored bottles? To cover up some of the fakes they sold as horseradish, including turnip mash and wood pulp.

★ **Runner-up:** The Mixer

In the 1600s the English drank a cocktail made from beer and chicken soup.

★ **And the Winner Is:** Ketchup

Care for a little ketchup on your burger? You might not if it was still made the way the English originally made it in the 1800s—without tomatoes.

What did they use instead? Puree of fish, lemons, and anchovies.

THE TOOTSIE ROLL TROPHY: FOR CANDY LIFE-SAVERS

During World War II, an American pilot named Frederick Arnold was shot down in the Sahara. Lost in the desert, he survived on the only thing he had to eat—the Tootsie Rolls in his pocket. The candy kept him going for three days.

Arnold met some desert nomads and convinced them to bring him to safety by trading his life for more Tootsie Rolls.

Let's see Life Savers match that.

THE OFF-THE-MENU PRIZE:
FOR FOODS WE NOW LOVE THAT NO ONE WOULD EAT WHEN THEY WERE FIRST SERVED

We are the only species that will continue to eat something we don't like the first time we try it. Eventually, we may develop a liking for what other animals leave behind if the initial taste revolts them. That's why you don't see mules smoking cigarettes, drinking whiskey, and eating olives.

★ **Third Place:** Hot Artichokes

Possession of artichokes was declared illegal in New York City during the mob Artichoke Wars of the 1920s. The Artichoke King, Ciro Terranova, tried to monopolize the thorny vegetable by intimidating other ditributors and cutting down plants in his rivals' artichoke fields.

To defuse the vegetable war, Fiorello La Guardia, mayor of New York City, declared the sale or possession of artichokes illegal. The ban lasted only one week because La Guardia loved artichokes too much to do without.

★ **Runner-up:** Potatoes

Yams were popular in colonial times. But Americans would not eat the common white potato in any form when it was brought over by Irish immigrants in the early eighteenth century.

Americans would have no fries with anything. No baked potatoes with sour cream and chives. No mashed, no hashed, no potato salad.

Potatoes were looked down upon, as were the Irish who ate them. Most Americans believed that potatoes were either bad for your health or were an aphrodisiac—or perhaps they thought aphrodisiacs were bad for your health.

It took Americans a long time to get over their prejudice toward the Irish and the potato. Meanwhile, they fed their potatoes to farm animals.

★ **And the Winner Is:** The Cup of Tar

The Arabs drank coffee as early as the sixteenth century. But the French and English wouldn't touch the stuff. Coffee reminded them of the hot tar that castle defenders poured on attacking soldiers. Brewing methods have improved since then.

THE NEAR BEER TROPHY: FOR TESTING THE THEORY THAT BEER LOVERS WILL DRINK ANYTHING

★ **Third Place:** Breakfast Beer

In Europe in the fifteenth and sixteenth centuries, people commonly had beer soup for breakfast.

★ **Runner-up:** Spud Suds

Early American colonists drank three kinds of beer that probably wouldn't challenge Bud for that King of Beer crown: pumpkin beer, potato beer, and persimmon beer.

On the other hand, pumpkin beer only cost a penny a quart.

★ **And the Winner Is:** Olde Frothingslosh

This short-lived beer had a slogan yet to be beat: "the stale ale with the foam on the bottom."

THE RING DING PRIZE FOR SILLY SNACK FOOD NAMES

We all bought into Twinkies, Yodels, and Sugar Smacks. Here are some winning snack names that lost out big on the supermarket shelves: Sesame Sillys, Onion Funions, Chipniks, Zooper Doopers, Tang-o-Chips, Kanga-Moo, Bokoo, Korkers, Hanky Panky, Onyums, and Dippy Canoes.

THE JARGON AWARDS, CHICKEN DIVISION:
HONORING THE CURIOUS LANGUAGE OF FACTORY FOOD

★ **Third Place:** On the Chicken Line

Because chickens are processed in huge numbers, they must be slaughtered and dismembered quickly if you are to be served on any day of the week what used to be reserved for Sunday dinner.

The factory workers who cut up the chickens are known as the "disassembly line."

★ **Runner-up:** Worn-out Chickens

"Chicken fatigue" does not refer to the tiring of chickens from running around with their heads chopped off. This curious phrase is the odd concern of chicken marketers for the modern palate, which tires of eating too much chicken more frequently than it does of eating too much beef.

★ **And the Winner Is:** Old Hens

Improving "the chicken note" is the manufacturing term for adding older hens (when their egg-laying services are no longer required) to the mix of younger chickens when creating processed chicken for nuggets, patties, chicken hot dogs, and other nonbony chicken creations.

The older hens add more flavor (the chicken note), while preparing them in this admixture obliterates the old birds' toughness.

CHARLEY THE TUNA'S MEMORIAL
GOOD TASTE AWARD: GOES TO RICE

Science knows best. We know this because scientists conducted a study to determine who knows best, and it turned out to be them.

But science can lead us into sneaky traps too. Take the story of rice.

Half the world's population depends on rice as their main source of food. Over the centuries, farmers have devised clever methods of growing rice throughout the Far East.

When Western scientists looked at those farming techniques, they thought; We can do a lot better. They bred hybrid varieties of rice that relied heavily on chemicals to increase yield and reduce the number of farm workers needed to bring in the crop. The results: more profit for corporate rice growers, more problems for actual people.

The new miracle rice spread around the world in the 1970s, replacing the old rice and the old methods of growing it. But over the years, the chemicals that protected the rice against disease and pests actually stimulated the diseases and pests to grow stronger.

Since farmers no longer used the old methods of controlling these problems, more chemicals were required to cope with the problems brought on by the chemicals in the first place.

One more problem: people didn't like the way the new rice tasted.

What could the rice industrialists say to that? What does taste have to do with science and industry? Who cares whether you actually like it? We've given you higher yield. Shut up and be thankful.

The Memorial Coffee Cup: Goes to Tea

In the years before the American Revolution, colonists primarily drank tea instead of coffee. But they were unhappy having to pay the British government a tax on their tea.

First, the colonists stopped drinking British tea and started drinking an American infusion known as Liberty Tea.

Then during the Revolutionary War, the colonists threw away all that tea, which was too British, and switched to coffee, even though it cost more. That's how coffee took over as king of the American table.

The International Table Manners Prize

★ **Third Place:** The Rice Bowl Challenge
Knocking over a man's rice bowl in China is a way of challenging him to a fight.

★ **Runner-up:** Kissy Kiss
In Argentina impatient diners summon the waiter by pursing their lips and making that kissy sound. We're still waiting for trendsetters to try that approach over here.

★ **And the Winner Is:** The Top Banana
In Bolivia people eat bananas with knives and forks. Too late to pitch the idea to Seinfeld or it might catch on in the U.S.A.

THE HIGH IRONY DIET PRIZE:
FOR GIVING US SOMETHING TO CHEW ON

If you've been to the supermarket lately, you'll appreciate this anonymous journalist's view on purchasing power: "Before the war I went to market with the money in my pocket and brought back my purchases in a basket. Now I take the money in the basket and bring the things home in my pocket."

The twist is, that's the Civil War the writer was talking about.

THE PHILOSOPHER'S CUP:
FOR PUTTING FOOD INTO THE BIGGER PICTURE

Some of the clearest observers on the state of restaurants are neither critics nor cooks, but philosophers.

"In large states, public education will always be mediocre," Friedrich Nietzsche observed, "for the same reason that in large kitchens the cooking is usually bad."

THE BREAKFAST OF CHAMPIONS FULL PLATE CUP:
FOR INNOVATIONS IN EATING

★ **Third Place:** The Batter's Breakfast

Ty Cobb was known as the meanest player in baseball, but also the best hitter.

When Cobb went on a forty-game hitting streak, he avoided jinxes by eating the same breakfast every day of the streak: six eggs, a dozen slices of bacon, four pieces of toast, a stack of flapjacks, a plate of grits, and a melon. Despite all that, he kept his playing weight at 175 pounds during the streak.

★ **Runner-up:** A Greek's Salad

The ancient Greek philosopher Aristippus of Cyrene practiced the system of pleasure-seeking called hedonism. He was such a gourmet that he would go into his garden and sprinkle salad dressing on his lettuce the day before he ate it for dinner.

★ **And the Winner Is:** The Daredevil's Doughnuts

Shipwreck Kelly was the man above town in Manhattan during the 1930s. As a famous flagpole sitter, Kelly once ate thirteen doughnuts while balancing upside down on his head at the end of a diving board that was hanging over the edge of the roof of a high-rise office building.

THE WAITRESSES' REVENGE UNION'S TURNING-THE-TABLE TROPHY

★ **Third Place:** The Meaty Stew

In 1995 a customer in an Australian restaurant sent back his dinner, claiming there wasn't enough meat in the stew. When the waitress brought the plate back out of the kitchen, it now had plenty of meat—she'd put a dead rat in the stew.

★ **Runner-up:** What's That Doing in My Soup?

In 1994 a customer and a waitress in a Bolivian restaurant got into a big dispute when he insisted he'd seen her sneeze into his soup. She pulled a pistol and forced him to eat the soup at gunpoint.

★ **And the Winner Is:** The Big Tipper

James Hill eventually became a millionaire railroad tycoon. But he started out working on the docks in Canada, where he was known for being exceptionally tight with a dollar.

One night he was having dinner in a restaurant with two dozen other dockworkers. When the meal ended, the men tried to divide up the bill and the tip. Hill asked the others if they would tip the waitress the same amount he did. They agreed, knowing he was the cheapest tipper among them.

Hill gave the waitress $20, and the other dockworkers felt honor-bound to do the same.

A week later, Hill and the waitress got married.

THE I'LL PASS PRIZE:
FOR THE FINAL WORD ON DIETS

Playwright Jean Kerr placed the eternal diet on the list of things that can be avoided if you work at it when she said, "I feel about airplanes the way I feel about diets. It seems to me that they are wonderful things for other people to go on."

Chapter 18

Winners of the Don't Miss America Beauty Con Test

Here she is, Miss America.

But seriously, folks, how can you miss America? It's right there.

Right here are winners of the Don't Miss America Beauty Con Test for people who keep trying to look better than nature intended people to look.

MISS IMMOBILITY

In the early 1900s fashionable women created a craze for the permanent in big-city beauty salons. To get one, your hair was pasted into asbestos tubes and you sat still for ten hours while your head was steamed in an iron helmet. Ten hours!

This system was eventually done away with in American beauty salons, but remained popular in less fashionable dictatorships around the world, where it was used on political prisoners.

Mr. Pumpkin Head

In the 1700s Puritan communities in New England passed a law requiring men to have their hair cut evenly all around their heads. They could also not wear sideburns, nor leave the back long.

New Englanders came to be known derisively as pumpkin heads because they looked like their hair had been cut using a pumpkin as a mold.

Mrs. Bolstered Hips

In eighteenth-century England, a man could legally annul his marriage if he discovered that his wife had tricked him into it through the use of cosmetics, perfumes, wigs, high heels, or "bolstered hips."

Mr. Nasty

In the early 1900s Darwinian scientists argued that women should not be allowed to use cosmetics because it thwarted the laws of evolution.

The scientists explained that cosmetically enhanced beauty tricked men into mating with women whom they would not have chosen had the pairing process gone according to natural selection.

Miss Incognito

In the late 1800s when beauty parlors were becoming common across the better parts of America, women wore veils when going there so they couldn't be identified and subjected to derision.

Mr. Macho Makeup Man

In the early twentieth century when women's cosmetics became big business, most of the makeup manufacturing companies were run by men.

To overcome the public perception that men in that business were effeminate, many of these marketing marvels pretended to be chemists or researchers in the cosmetic sciences. That's why they always wore lab coats when making public appearances.

Mr. Smellgood

Now you can buy your deodorant at the grocery store, the drugstore, or other places that hope you'll smell good the next time you come in.

But in the 1920s as underarm deodorant became a marketer's dream, it was first sold door to door.

Mr. and Mrs. Fur Permit

In the thirteenth century the ruling class of France passed a dress code for the entire country. Required dress for the poorer classes? Oh, any old thing will do.

Not surprisingly, only members of the aristocracy were permitted to wear gold, jewels, or furs. Anyone else who dressed illegally in furs could be sent to prison.

I think Beverly Hills still has that city ordinance.

Ms. Worth It

In ancient times Byzantium silk was so rare, it was worth more than jewels. In a palace power play, Cleopatra refused to wear anything but Byzantium silk, thus forcing the Egyptian empire to spend one of the world's largest fortunes on her clothes.

Mr. Whisper

In the early 1800s in the polite society of the Eastern states, it was considered a display of improper breeding to refer to this particular piece of clothing. So they were called "unexpressibles."

Can you guess what they were? No, not underwear. Pants or trousers, also known as "unwhisperables."

Mr. Panties

Forbes, not noted as a sports or fashion magazine, sunk its investigative teeth into the issue of male chafe with this advice to men who jog: take off the jockstrap and wear women's panties under your shorts because they prevent that irritating jogger's chafe.

Miss Smudge Smile

In the 1800s proper Americans whitened their teeth with a mixture of honey and ground-up charcoal.

MR. TRENDSETTER

Celebrities may be different than you and me, but not always better dressed.

When consumer advocate Ralph Nader was studying at Princeton, he decided to launch a protest against conformist clothing. How did he rebel against authority? He wore a bathrobe to class.

MS. SPIRITS

Earrings were originally designed to block evil spirits from getting inside your head through your ears. Precious metals and stones were hung there for defense, not adornment.

MS. BALDIE

When a woman mocked St. Leufredus's baldness, he turned her and all her family bald.

MR. FLAW

Photographer Diane Arbus made a career out of picturing people in their distortions. She had an eye for the frustrations of the cosmetic attempt. "You see someone on the street," she said, "and essentially what you notice about them is the flaw."

GREAT MOMENTS IN ADVANCED TRIVIA, MISS AMERICA DIVISION

Fans of the Miss America Pageant know it's not all about looks, talent, poise, and the ability to smile no matter how much your feet are hurting. It's also about some really odd Miss America trivia.

1. Miss America winners with odd names:

Venus Ramey (1944), BeBe Shopp (1948), Yolande Betbeze (1951), Vonda Kay Van Dyke (1965), Tawney Elaine Godin (1976), Kylene Barker (1979), Kellye Cash (1987), Debbye Turner (1990) and Leanza Cornett (1993).

2. The Anne Phenomenon. An odd string of Miss America winners weren't named Anne but had Anne as a middle name.

No Annes at all from 1921 through 1958. Then came the wave of Anne winners: Mary Ann Mobley (1959), Jane Anne Jayroe (1967), Judith Anne Ford (1969), Pamela Anne Eldred (1970), Phyllis Ann George (1971), Terry Anne Meeuwsen (1973), and Rebecca Ann King (1974). None since.

Ms. Superhuman

Writer Germaine Greer hoped to liberate women from the chains of the beauty industry. She questioned the futility this way: "Is it too much to ask that women be spared the daily struggle for superhuman beauty in order to offer it to the caresses of a sub-humanly ugly mate?"

Mr. Role Model

Dennis Rodman stands alone, and not just by personality. He was a dominant rebounder in the NBA for years. But unlike other star athletes, he wasn't afraid to be a role model—well, a model.

After basketball, Rodman posed in leather hot pants for a magazine, then topped that stunt by posing nude for another magazine.

Mr. Hope

"In the factory we make cosmetics," makeup magnate Charles Revson said. "In the drugstore we sell hope."

Mr. Prussian

Kaiser Wilhelm II of Prussia was rather fond of military uniforms. He kept four hundred of them on hand for his personal use, and redesigned the uniforms of the German army thirty-seven times in seventeen years.

You have to admire a dictator who if he doesn't get it right the first thirty-six times, then convinces himself he will get it right the thirty-seventh time.

Great Moments in the Vision of Beauty

1. Chinese proverb—When you have only two pennies left in the world, buy a loaf of bread with one and a lily with the other.

2. From writer Henry Miller—"The moment one gives close attention to anything, even a blade of grass, it becomes a mysterious, awesome, indescribably magnificent world in itself."

3. From critic John Ruskin—"Remember that the most beautiful things in the world are the most useless; peacocks and lilies, for example."

4. From songwriter Oscar Hammerstein II—"Do you love me because I'm beautiful? Or am I am beautiful because you love me?"

5. From philosopher Ralph Waldo Emerson—"What is a weed? A plant whose virtues have not yet been discovered."

Ms. Doodler

In the 1950s the popularity of the Miss America contest spawned many other beauty contests, including the National College Queen Pageant.

Contestants, who were all college students, competed not only in the skill of wearing bathing suits, but in such other university-related talents as how well they could doodle, cook burgers, iron blouses, and pour coffee for judges.

Ms. Glamour

"Any girl can look glamorous," the glamorous movie star Hedy Lamarr advised. "All you have to do is stand still and look stupid."

Ms. Highlights

The actor Maurice Chevalier who played so many romantic Frenchmen in Hollywood movies said of off-screen romantic possibilities: "Many a man has fallen in love with a girl in a light so dim he would not have chosen a suit by it."

Ms. Snow Wear

A wealthy Frenchwoman of the Victorian Era and proper mind-set left an endowment in her will to buy clothes for naked French snowmen. Naked French peasants were on their own.

Ms. Recycler

Plenty of moose in Alaska. That means plenty of moose dung. What to do? Make earrings out of it, of course. Alaska shops sell thousands of moose-dung earrings each year.

Mr. Max II

Max Factor, the Hollywood cosmetician who marketed a famous line of beauty products in the 1920s, named his son Frank. When his father died, Frank changed his name to Max so as not to complicate the company's advertising campaign.

Mr. Style Setter

When matinee idol Rudolph Valentino bought a home in Bel Air, he painted the rooms black and decorated them with black furniture.

Mr. Bald, Fat, and Ugly

Anchor Connie Chung explained how television news works when she said, "Men are allowed to be bald, fat and ugly and still deliver the news. There are no bald, fat and ugly women delivering the news."

Chapter 19

The So-So Housekeeping Awards:
For Families of Winners

There are more guides telling us how to be good parents than there are good parents. The So-So Housekeeping Awards honor those people who have faced the tough quandaries—like, should you lock your kids in the safe—and other family issues that Dr. Spock never thought of.

THE SAFETY PRIZE: GOES TO THE COUPLE
WHO BURGLARY-PROOFED THE BABY

In 2004 a Nebraska couple decided to convert the walk-in safe in their new home into a nursery—then proceeded to lock their baby inside the safe.

Yes, they had a good excuse. When they'd bought the house, the previous owners told them the safe's lock had been disabled.

A locksmith opened the door and disconnected the lock. To be on the safe side, the parents took the door off the hinges before putting baby down for another nap.

ALL IN THE FAMILY PRIZE:
FOR UPHOLDING UNUSUAL FAMILY TRADITIONS

★ **Third Place:** The Youngest Son

Benjamin Franklin was the youngest son of the youngest son. So was his grandfather, great-grandfather, and great-great-grandfather.

★ **Runner-up:** The Fifty Youngest Sons

Defying the overpopulation pessimists, King Sobhuza II of Swaziland fathered two hundred children with seventy wives.

★ **And the Winner Is:** The Five Hundred Youngest Sons

An Irish bull named Bendalls Adema sired more than two hundred thousand offspring in the 1960s and 1970s.

THE STAGE MOTHER PRIZE: FOR PARENTS WHO
GAVE THEIR FAMOUS KIDS THAT EXTRA SHOVE

★ **Third Place:** Funny Reversal

When *Austin Powers* star Mike Myers was growing up, his mother considered him the least funny of her three sons.

He wanted to become a comic and an actor, but she advised against it. "Michael, you know how there are funny people? Well you're not one of them."

★ **Runner-up:** Early Drawings

While pregnant, one expectant mother wanted her baby to grow up to become an architect. Before the boy was born, she hung drawings of cathedrals in the baby's room to inspire him. The boy grew up to become architect Frank Lloyd Wright.

★ **And the Winner Is:** Ancient Inspiration

She was a piano teacher. While pregnant, she decided to instill a love of culture and beauty in her baby by meditating upon a Greek statue before retiring each night. The boy grew up to become pianist Percy Grainger.

THE PREPARENTING AWARD:
FOR OLD, ODD IDEAS IN CHILD RAISING

★ **Third Place:** Launching the Kids

To launch a new ship, people smash a bottle of champagne across the bow, although others consider that a waste of a good drink. The ancients smashed a boy when launching a ship, believing a child sacrificed would appease the angry gods of the sea.

★ **Runner-up:** Early Training

St. Francis Xavier said that if he could educate children until they were seven years old, anyone could take them afterward and the child would remain good. In the sixteenth century, the English military started training boys at the age of seven to be soldiers.

★ **And the Winner Is:** Parental Protection

Archduchess Marie Louise of Austria was so sheltered as a child that no male animals were allowed within her sight. Her royal parents protected her from everything but Napoleon. They married her off to the conqueror of Europe. So much for the concept of sheltering.

THE CHIP OFF THE OLD BLOCK PRIZE:
FOR GETTING KIDS OFF TO AN EARLY, IF UNUSUAL, START

★ **Third Place:** The Ear Stretcher

The composer Charles Ives got an early start in music because his father George, a music teacher and bandleader, led his children in experimental music drills. George attempted to stretch his kids' musical ear by having them sing in one key while he played the accompaniment in another key.

★ **Runner-up:** The Wolf Boy

St. Ailbe, patron saint of wolves, was raised by a wolf after his father threw him away as a baby.

★ **And the Winner Is:** The Baby Champ

When he was not quite two years old, future boxing champ Muhammad Ali clipped his mom by accident and knocked out one of her teeth.

THE FEEDING AND CARING OF JUNIOR PRIZE

★ **Third Place:** The Fat States

Mississippi has the most overweight kids in the nation. Arkansas is number two and closing fast, with one in four school kids overweight.

In 2004 Arkansas legislators introduced a law to weigh schoolkids. To keep the kids from being humiliated in front of their classmates, school nurses wouldn't announce their weight out loud and the kids would stand on the scale backward so they couldn't see their own weight.

The idea was to compile statistics and give a weighty report card to the parents. Can you imagine having to get your fatty report card signed before you could go out for a burger and fries?

★ **Runner-up:** Baby Tonic

In the 1800s drug companies sold a tonic called Baby's Friend for mothers to give their infants who had trouble sleeping. The tonic contained morphine, which did make the babies sleep but also turned them into addicts. How do you say no to drugs if you're too young to speak?

★ **And the Winners Are:** English Judges

In the 1800s English judges were not themselves judged. Many of them sentenced poor children to be hung for minor crimes. In 1801 a seven-year-old boy was hung for stealing a spoon.

THE PRIZE DAD PRIZE:
JUST FOR BEING DAD

★ **Third Place:** The Sew-and-Sew

Isaac Singer made a fortune manufacturing his sewing machines. He also had innumerable affairs and fathered many children, all of whom he refused to support.

★ **Runner-up:** The Moose's Dad

Bill Skowron, first baseman for the New York Yankees when they won one World Series after another in the Mickey Mantle era, was nicknamed Moose—but not because he was big and strong, which he was.

His father gave him the Moose nickname when Bill was a kid because he thought the youngster looked like the Italian dictator Mussolini.

★ **And the Winner Is:** The Absentee Dad

According to trainer Cus D'Amato, heavyweight boxing champ Mike Tyson had one advantage over other boxers. D'Amato claimed that Tyson became a champion because he didn't have a father around giving him bad training advice.

THE DI'S TRAINING RIBBON:
FOR ANCIENT SERGEANTS

In Sparta teenage boys were prepared for the military through whipping contests. The boys would gather in the public square, where they were group-whipped. Last boy standing was the winner.

You know what they used to say in ancient Sparta: spare the whip, spoil the child.

PRIZE DOGS PRIZE

From 1954 to 1978, the Dog Heroes of the Year Award for saving the lives of children went to seven collies, seven German shepherds, and five St. Bernards.

In comparison, miniature poodles won one.

M IS FOR THE MONEY PRIZE

Hetty Green was one of the richest landowners in nineteenth-century New York City, hoarding millions she never spent. But when her young son dropped a coin in the street, she forced him to spend all night searching for it as she carried a lantern up and down the sidewalks of New York.

THE SPACED-OUT AWARD:
FOR SAYING NO WHEN YOU SHOULD SAY YES

Mars Candy Company, the M&M's people, said no when director Steven Spielberg asked them if E.T. could love M&M's in his upcoming movie for kids. No M&M's for creatures from outer space.

So E.T. fell for Reese's Pieces instead. So did millions of E.T. fans.

THE POINTLESS PRIZE, FOR DOING SOMETHING INCREDIBLY DIFFICULT FOR NO APPARENT REASON AT ALL:
GOES TO "HARRY POTTER AND THE GREEK PROFESSOR"

A classics teacher in England, Andrew Wilson, was hired to translate the three-hundred-page kids' book *Harry Potter and the Sorcerer's Stone* into ancient Greek despite the fact that there are no ancient Greeks to read it.

The few classical scholars who read ancient Greek fluently are the least likely people to read a book that is of dubious interest to adults in modern English.

It was, according to Wilson, the longest piece of writing to be translated into ancient Greek in 1,500 years. Perhaps they'll make it a regular event and translate "Harry Potter Goes Hawaiian" into ancient Greek 1,500 years from now.

THE KID PROTECTION PRIZE

In 1998 the administration at a St. Louis high school stopped the school band from playing the Jefferson Airplane's song "White Rabbit" because the lyrics included drug references. The school band was playing an instrumental version that had no lyrics.

THE ROCK 'N' ROLL WAS ALWAYS DANGEROUS AWARD

Rap music has been hit hard by protestors upset with its often violent and abusive lyrics. Such is the history of rock 'n' roll. In 1959 the Coasters' hit song "Charlie Brown" was banned in England because of its lyrics about kids "throwing spitballs."

THE TOO TOUGH TO BE A PARENT AWARD

★ **Third Place:** The Writer

"It's frightening to think that you mark your children merely by being yourself," writer Simone de Beauvoir said. "It seems unfair. You can't assume the responsibility for everything you do, or don't do."

★ **Runner-up:** The Rocker

"To be a conscious parent and really look to that little being's mental and physical health is a responsibility which most of us, including me, avoid most of the time because it's too hard."

Who admitted that? Ex-Beatle John Lennon.

★ **And the Winner Is:** The Movie Star

"If you have never been hated by your child," movie star Bette Davis said, "you have never been a parent."

THE AVUNCULAR ADVICE PRIZE

Writer Mark Twain offered this advice to children: "Always do right. This will gratify some people and astonish the rest."

THE PARENTS VS. THE DEVIL PRIZE:
GOES TO INDIA

In 2003 the parents of a nine-year-old girl from India thought she was under the spell of a devil. They had her cured by marrying the girl to a dog.

No doubt many women feel that might explain their own marriages.

THE TOO LATE TO DIAPER AWARD:
GOES TO FAMOUS PEOPLE WHO WAITED
TILL THEY COULD AFFORD PLENTY OF
CHILD CARE BEFORE THEY HAD CHILDREN

1. Famous men who fathered children when they were over forty—actors Humphrey Bogart, Clark Gable, Charlie Chaplin, Edward G. Robinson, and Ronald Colman; writers Joseph Conrad, C. P. Snow, and Alfred Tennyson; painters Mark Rothko and Fra Filippo Lippi; robber baron Leland Stanford.

2. Famous women who had babies late on the biological clock— artist Yoko Ono and model Jean Shrimpton (both at thirty-seven); actresses Diana Rigg (at thirty-nine), Claudia Cardinale (at forty), Lucille Ball (at forty-two), and Ursula Andress (at forty-four).

Chapter 20

The Second Voice of God
and Other Prize-Winning
Things We Believe

The Church of the Eternally Confused presents its Spreading the Faith prizes, for people who have found surprising flexibility in the name of the Lord.

THE SURPRISING JESUS AWARDS:
FOR NEW WAYS TO CAPITALIZE ON CHRIST

★ **Third Place:** Star Jesus

Mel Gibson's movie *The Passion of the Christ* raised religious controversies when it was released in 2004. It also raised eyebrows at a movie theater in Rome, Georgia, when the tickets printed for the film were coded with the number 666 (the "mark of the beast," according to the Book of Revelations).

The theater manager claimed the number was a coincidence and blamed the mistake on the computer system. You didn't have to be a believer to agree that computers are controlled by the devil.

★ **Runner-up:** Toy Jesus

In the 1950s the Ideal Toy Company marketed the Most Wonderful Story doll. But the marketing execs failed to consider what kids do with their toys—toss them in the closet, tear them to pieces, toss them to the dog.

Would religious parents be comfortable with that kind of treatment of a Baby Jesus doll? They would not, and the toy didn't sell.

★ **And the Winner Is:** Bilingual Jesus

When the Texas legislature was looking into bilingual issues, the state's former governor "Farmer Jim" Ferguson offered this testimony: "If English was good enough for Jesus Christ, it's good enough for the schoolchildren of Texas."

THE POWER OF THE CHURCH AWARD:
FOR ADVANCED METHODS OF SPREADING THE WORD

★ **Third Place:** The Viking Strategy

St. Olaf of Norway was an eleventh-century Viking who converted to Christianity with a vengeance. When other Vikings resisted conversion, he persuaded them to see the light by burning down their houses, chopping off their hands, and putting out their eyes. Good arguments, Olaf.

★ **Runner-up:** The Borne-Again Pilot

Many pilots who have survived close scrapes come out of it feeling that God is their copilot. But one American Airlines pilot apparently felt that Jesus was his ticket agent.

The pilot offered an original alternative to the in-flight movie during a 2004 flight from L.A. to New York. He asked all the Christians on the plane to raise their hands, then suggested the other passengers discuss religion with the faithful.

Some passengers grew nervous that the pilot was intending to take them to Jesus a little sooner than they were prepared to go. But the flight landed on time and in New York, which few people have confused with heaven.

An airline spokesman said the pilot's actions fell "along the lines of a personal level of sharing that may not be appropriate for one of our employees to do while on the job."

However, the pilot may have opened up new dimensions of air travel. "Good morning, Christians and the damned. We realize you have no choice when you fly, so thank the Lord you're flying with us. Now if you look out the window to the left of the aircraft, you will see that we're either passing over the Grand Canyon or under the Pearly Gates."

★ **And the Winner Is:** The Other Voice of God

When Celestine V became pope in 1294, he took his vows more literally than previous popes. Celestine lived in a humble cell built inside the papal palace. When he began to give away the riches of the church to poor people, he upset the cardinals, who felt that the meek should inherit the earth but not necessarily their part of it.

To save the church from the pope, Cardinal Benedetto drilled a hole in the wall of the pope's cell. At night, Benedetto whispered to the pope, claiming to be the voice of the Holy Ghost and demanding that Celestine abdicate. He did, and the wealth of the church was saved.

Most Convincing
Advertisement for Heaven

In 2004 Canada rolled out a new ad campaign to attract tourists, headlining it: "So unbelievably beautiful it's not just a vacation. It's practice for the afterlife."

This came as some comfort to people expecting to go to a hotter, less scenic locale.

For those who were expecting heaven without the shopping in Montreal option, Canada's revelation ran contrary to the claim that you can't take it with you. If heaven is run by Canadians, apparently you *have* to take it with you because there will be charges. Also, plenty of golf in between the harp solos.

The Anti-Vacuumists Award:
For explaining why nothing can't exist

St. Robert Bellarmine, a Jesuit scholar, declared that Galileo's claim that the Earth revolves around the sun was as "erroneous as to claim that Jesus was not born of a virgin."

According to church scholars, Galileo broke another of God's laws when he experimented with vacuums. Not the dirt-sucking kind, the nothing kind.

The Church maintained that since God was everywhere, a vacuum could not possibly exist.

THE WHY IS THAT CUTE LITTLE EASTER BUNNY BLEEDING, MOM? AWARD: FOR ORIGINALITY IN PAGEANTRY

In 2004 a Pennsylvania church put on an Easter pageant that surprised parents who brought their young children to the show, expecting a more traditional egg hunt.

Instead, a member of the congregation wearing a rabbit suit was whipped to represent the story of Christ's crucifixion, leaving parents to explain to youngsters why the Easter bunny was being beaten up.

AND ANOTHER THING AWARD: FOR ORIGINALITY IN CONVERSATIONS WITH GOD

Marlon Brando worked with Frank Sinatra in the movie *Guys and Dolls* and felt that his costar had a unique relationship with his Maker. "He's the kind of guy that when he dies, he's going up to heaven and give God a bad time for making him bald," Brando said.

THE IMMACULATE PHONE CALL PRIZE: FOR REPORTS FROM THE AFTERLIFE

The British Lord Desborough was surprised to find his obituary in the London *Times* one morning, then realized the newspaper must have gotten it wrong because it was Lord Bessborough who had died.

When Desborough phoned the paper for a correction, he introduced himself to an editor and said, "You've published my obituary this morning."

"I see," the editor said, "and where did you say you were calling from?"

THE DOUBTER'S PRIZE

"Religious ideas are inflammatory in a way that I find difficult to understand," the English writer Quentin Crisp said. "There are very few wars over the theory of relativity."

THE THINKERS' PRIZE

★ **Third Place:** Psychologist William James
"Religion is a monumental chapter in the history of human egotism."

★ **Runner-up:** Writer Jonathan Swift
"We have just enough religion to make us hate, but not enough to make us love one another."

★ **And the Winner Is:** Writer H. L. Mencken
"The cosmos is a gigantic flywheel making 10,000 revolutions a minute. Man is a sick fly taking a dizzy ride on it. Religion is the theory that the wheel was designed and set spinning to give him the ride."

THE PEW AWARD: IN RECOGNITION THAT NO SLEIGHT IS TOO SMALL TO GO UNNOTICED

Pews in churches were originally roped-off seats reserved for the rich families in the congregation. Ordinary people (the kind Jesus used to preach to) weren't allowed to sit in the church pews.

THE SAINTS ALIVE AWARD:
FOR THE BEST OF BUDDIES

★ **Third Place:** The Saint and the Lions
When St. Paul the Hermit died, two lions dug his grave.

★ **Runner-up:** The Saint and the Croc
St. Pachomius of Egypt crossed the Nile River by riding on the back of a crocodile. Other people have crossed rivers this way, but not all the way across.

★ **And the Winners Are:** The Saint and the Well-Dressed Eagle
To escape from hunters, a bear stole clothes from St. Ghislain. But an eagle led the saint to the bear's cave so he could get his clothes back.

THE HOLY MONEY MEDAL

Preacher Jerry Falwell clarified God's position on why some people are rich and some aren't when he said, "Material wealth is God's way of blessing people who put Him first."

Jesus had a different opinion on the subject, but then he wasn't rich.

GREAT MOMENTS IN ODD BELIEFS

These superstitions were good enough to mess up the lives of our ancestors, and they're good enough to mess up ours too.

1. In ancient Europe no one wanted to be first across a new bridge. People believed that after a bridge was built the first person to cross it would die. But they apparently didn't stick to their beliefs since all bridges were crossed.

2. Centuries ago, if a man started on a journey but forgot something and returned home to get it, he first sat down in the middle of the road and counted backward from seven. The backward counting confused the devil.

People held a lot of contradictory notions about Satan. Even though they believed the devil was one of the most powerful creatures in all creation, they also believed he couldn't count backward.

3. In the mountains of North Carolina, it was considered good luck to be passed by a girl with red hair riding a white mule.

This superstition didn't work as well in L.A. or New York City, unless you passed a girl with red hair wearing white mules.

4. In England it's considered a bad idea to ask two people to help you make the bed in the morning. Menage a trois you may, but pull up the covers yourself. For if three make a bed, one will surely die. Household chores can be a high-risk occupation.

5. In Scotland it's considered unlucky for women to sing while baking bread.

6. If you want a good night's sleep, don't turn your mattress around on a Sunday. Plus, when you make the bed in the morning, don't let anything interrupt you until you're done.

7. If it's the middle of May and you need a new broom, wait till June. According to an old superstition, brooms bought in May sweep the family away.

8. Unlucky brooms were not confined to the house. Olde English shoppe keepers wouldn't sweep the sidewalk in the morning, worried they would sweep away customers.

9. In parts of England it's considered unlucky to tell anyone how old you are. Parts of Hollywood too.

10. To get rid of warts, a person would rub the wart with a stone, then drop the stone at a crossroad.

11. A woman thinking about marriage will dream of the man to be her mate the night before the feast day of St. Agnes (January 21)—if she first eats nothing for twenty-four hours, then eats an egg with salt before going to sleep.

Who started this rumor, the National Egg and Salt Board?

12. In ancient Scotland a couple looking for good fortune to shine on their marriage had the ceremony performed not by a priest but by a village blacksmith, shoemaker, or rat catcher.

Rat catcher? Do you take this rat to love, honor, and obey?

13. In the Dark Ages, Europeans believed that bees hummed the Hundredth Psalm on Christmas Eve to celebrate the birth of Christ.

No report on what Jewish bees hummed.

14. People once believed that toothaches were caused by a worm that burrowed into the tooth beneath the gum.

15. In the 1800s the concept that life was created through spontaneous generation became a popular notion. People became convinced that mice were created, not by other mice, but as a by-product of cheese going bad.

16. When Hawaii was ruled by kings, people were forbidden to let their shadows fall upon the palace grounds.

17. During the Great Depression, hoboes carried pebbles in their pocket. When they entered a hobo camp, they threw the pebbles on the ground to let everyone know they were real hobos, not bums.

HIT AND MYTH AWARDS: FOR STRANGE THINGS ANCIENT ROMANS BELIEVED ABOUT ANIMALS

★ **Third Place:** Bird Lights

There were birds who would guide you through the dark by lighting up their tails at night.

★ **Runner-up:** Flying Snakes

In distant lands there were flying snakes and people with the heads of dogs.

★ **And the Winner Is:** Golden Ants

In Ethiopia there were giant ants that mined for gold.

ANCIENT DOCTOR AWARDS:
FOR THE CLEVER MEDICAL BELIEFS OF THE MIDDLE AGES

★ **Third Place:** The Key to Fevers
To bring down a fever, sick people held a metal key in their hand.

★ **Runner-up:** Shutting the Door on Headaches
To cure headaches, people coated their door hinges with vinegar.

★ **And the Winner Is:** The Middle Finger Detector
Doctors stirred medicine with the middle finger of their left hand. They believed that was the one finger that could detect impurities in the medicine.

GOLD STARS: FOR SAINTS WHO WERE
NOT JUST HOLY BUT CURIOUSLY TALENTED

1. St. Sebald of Germany could burn icicles as firewood.

2. St. Peter Claver of Spain could fix broken eggs.

3. St. Fridolin of Ireland could spot holy remains buried under the ground.

4. St. Giles of France had the power of handling and shipping. While visiting the pope in Rome, he was given two massive doors for his church. Instead of sending them overland, Giles tossed them into the river Arno and commanded them to float back to Provence, which they did. Federal Express has yet to offer this kind of service.

5. St. Joseph of Cupertino had passenger power. Not only could he fly, he carried fellow friars on his back when he flew from place to place.

6. St. Finnbar of Ireland had the unusual power to make trees bear hazelnuts upon command. He would harvest them by commanding the nuts to fall into his lap.

Chapter 21

The Going Out in Style Awards: Innovations in Death

If you have to go—and apparently you do—you can still win a door prize on your way out with one of our Going Out in Style Awards.

THE UP CUP: FOR LOOKING ON THE BRIGHT SIDE OF DEATH, GOES TO MR. POPULARITY

"It is difficult to be thoroughly popular," the English actor Herbert Beerbohm Tree pointed out, "until one is quite dead."

FINAL TRIBUTE TROPHIES: FOR EVERLASTING THOUGHTFULNESS

★ **Third Place:** That Icelandic Sense of Humor

In 1993 a funeral home in Iceland got a little carried away with the timing when a man died on Christmas Day. For the funeral, the undertaker dressed the man in a fake white beard and a Santa suit.

★ **Runner-up:** That French Connection

In 1977 two pet lovers wanted to have their dogs buried with them. But French law prohibited animals from being buried in cemeteries intended for people. So the two women bought plots for themselves in the pet cemetery.

★ **And the Winner Is:** That British Diet

Writer George Bernard Shaw requested that his funeral procession should be joined by chickens, sheep, an ox, and an aquarium. Why? As the animals way of saying thanks for his being a vegetarian.

THE WHOLE PACKAGE PRIZE:
FOR THOUGHTS ABOUT THE LIFE YOU CAN'T HAVE WITHOUT DEATH

★ **Third Place:** English Composer and Writer Samuel Butler
"Life is one long process of getting tired."

★ **Runner-up:** French Poet Charles Baudelaire
"Life is a hospital in which every patient is possessed by the desire of changing his bed. One would prefer to suffer near the fire. Another is certain he would get well if he were by the window."

★ **And the Winner Is:** American Writer Fran Lebowitz
"Life is something to do when you can't get to sleep."

GREAT MOMENTS IN THE
PURSUIT OF DUMB WAYS TO DIE

The Semigrim Reaper, not as grim as he used to be, helps peo-ple who aren't satisfied that life is going to take care of itself to find ingenious early exits.

1. A French gourmet was training to break the world record for snail eating in 1979. To warm up, he ate seventy-two escargot in less than three minutes. Then he died.

2. José de los Santos was a nineteenth-century Spanish bull-fighter who had one too many fights. Fighting a bull one hot after-noon, he was close to being skewered on the bull's horns when he dived over a fence—and was skewered on his own sword.

3. The sixteenth-century scientist Girolamo Cardano was also a famous astrologer. He claimed that the stars predicted he would die on September 21, 1576.

On that day, Cardano, healthy and without an enemy in sight, decided that his astrological prediction could not be mistaken. So he committed suicide.

4. Li Po was an eighth-century poet with the dreamy inclina-tions enjoyed by other poets down through the ages. But few ended their lives quite as poetically as Li Po, who was enchanted by the moon's reflection on a lake. He leaned over the edge of his boat to kiss that reflection, tumbled over the side, and drowned.

5. Bobby Leech was an American daredevil who rode a bar-rel over Niagara Falls in 1911. That stunt has killed plenty of risk

addicts. But Leech survived the drop, although he did suffer many broken bones.

The stunt earned Leech a world lecture tour. At a stop in New Zealand, he slipped on a banana peel, banged his head on the street, and died.

6. Great military men lead their troops into battle. Great military men who survive those battles lead their troops carefully. Then there was General John Sedgwick, who commanded Union forces at the battle of Spotsylvania Courthouse during the Civil War.

To encourage his men to stand firm against the Confederate charge, Sedgwick rode his horse to the front and shouted, "They couldn't hit an elephant at this dist . . ."

No elephants were hurt in the battle, but apparently the Confederates could hit rash officers without any problem.

7. Yousouf Ishmaelo was a Turkish wrestling champion who made a lot of money on a U.S. tour in 1897. Ishmaelo took his winnings in gold, which he wore in a belt when he boarded a ship for the journey home.

When his ship, *Le Bourgogne,* rammed another ship and started to sink, Ishmaelo jumped overboard. Even though he was a strong swimmer, he drowned because he refused to take off the gold belt.

8. Lupe Velez was an early film star on the downside of her Hollywood career when she decided to end it all.

Ever the star, she dressed and made up for the photos that she knew would play big in the L.A. papers after her body was discovered.

Looking marvelous, Lupe swallowed some pills and lay down on her bed. She made one miscalculation—the pills made her nauseous. When Lupe Velez was discovered dead the next day, it wasn't in bed. She was riding the porcelain bus.

9. French soldiers under Napoleon were marching through the Syrian desert in 1799 to attack the enemy. Desperate with thirst, the soldiers drank from a stream infested with leeches. The leeches latched onto the soldiers' throats and choked hundreds of them to death.

10. Hart Crane seemed to have things going his way. He was a writer successful with critics and book buyers and had won a Guggenheim Fellowship.

But taking a ship from Mexico back to the United States in 1932, Crane surprised the other passengers when he suddenly said, "Good-bye, everybody," and jumped overboard. He sank, leaving only traces of why he did it.

11. In 1909 George Hensley, a Tennessee preacher, began handling rattlesnakes with his congregation as part of their worship. The preacher died forty-six years later from one of many snake bites.

The religious handling of snakes is still practiced in some churches, which means more people insist on stirring up the snakes who are expert at defense but rarely go charging after people.

12. In the 1800s American mothers put copper coins into the kitchen pickling crocks with the cucumbers because the copper turned pickles a deep, pleasing green. Unfortunately, the coins also killed people who ate the poisoned pickles.

CELEBRITY DEATH LOTTO WINNERS,
HONORING FATAL COINCIDENCES OF THE FAMOUS

★ **Third Place:** The Brontës

A talented family, the Brontës were not good candidates for a thirty-year mortgage.

Anne Brontë had two books published by the time she was only twenty-nine. But then she was ever only twenty-nine—that's the age at which she died.

Her sister Emily published *Wuthering Heights* when she was twenty-nine but died the next year. Their brother Branwell was a painter who died when he was thirty-one. Their sister Charlotte published *Jane Eyre* at thirty-one and managed to live until she set a Brontë sibling longevity record of thirty-nine.

★ **Runner-up:** The Picassos

In life Pablo Picasso had strange impacts on the people closest to him. In death, also.

On the same day as Picasso's funeral, his grandson Pablito committed suicide by poisoning himself. Four years later, Picasso's mistress and model Marie-Therese Walter hung herself. Nine years after that, Picasso's widow committed suicide by shooting herself.

★ **And the Winners Are:** The Communists

Communist leader Karl Marx had two daughters who committed suicide. Communist leader Leon Trotsky's daughter committed suicide. So did Communist leader Josef Stalin's wife.

THE FINAL INSPIRATION PRIZE:
FOR NEVER GROWING UP

As a child, Peter Llewellyn Davies served as inspiration for writer J. M. Barrie when he created the boy who never grew up, Peter Pan.

Kenneth Grahame was inspired by his little son Alastair (called Mouse) to invent the stories that became *The Wind in the Willow*.

As adults, both youthful inspirations killed themselves by stepping into the path of an oncoming train.

THE OVERKILL PRIZE:
FOR FATAL OBSESSIONS

★ **Third Place:** For the Love of Art

The Dutch artist Rembrandt married a rich heiress to finance his paintings. When she died and he needed more money, he sold the tomb over her grave.

★ **Runner-up:** For Love of the King

English revolutionary Oliver Cromwell overthrew the king in the seventeenth century. When the Royalists regained power after Cromwell's death, they felt they hadn't been given adequate opportunity to exercise the royal prerogative for revenge.

So they exhumed Cromwell's body, hanged the corpse from the gallows, and beheaded him.

★ **And the Winner Is:** For the Guards

A death row inmate in an Oklahoma prison managed to steal enough sleeping pills to commit suicide the night before he was due to be executed for murder.

Guards found him unconscious in his cell. They took him to the prison hospital and revived him. Then they led him back to death row and executed him.

THE SHORT-LIVED CUP:
FOR PEOPLE UNCLEAR ON THE CONCEPT OF DEATH

★ **Third Place:** The Horse You Rode Out On

During the French Revolution, radicals dug up the body of St. Joan of Lestonnac, then threw her back into a grave with a horse.

★ **Runner-up:** The Restless Corpse

After St. Mathurin was buried in Rome, he rose from his grave and went back to his hometown in France, then reburied himself there.

★ **And the Winner Is:** The Temporary Leader

Mother Ann Lee, an eighteenth-century English mystic, converted many Americans to the visionary Shaker faith. Lee, who presented herself as God the Mother, preached total abstinence even within marriage.

It was pointed out to Lee that total abstinence would limit the faithful since there would be no later Shakers to follow their leaders. Mother Lee explained that the world was going to end soon anyway. Therefore, they didn't need another generation of Shakers.

That was in 1780, a slight miscalculation which might have upset future Shakers had there been any.

THE FED-UP PRIZE:
FOR ODD CONNECTIONS BETWEEN DEATH AND FOOD

★ **Third Place:** Too Much Molasses

In 1919 twenty-one people died in Boston in a molasses flood when thousands of gallons poured through a street, creating a thick wave as high as a two-story house.

★ **Runner-up:** Too Much Beer

In 1814 in London nine people drowned in beer when a brewery spilled 3,500 barrels, flooding nearby houses with suds.

★ **And the Winner Is:** Too Much Chocolate

In 1973 a man who worked for a Swedish candy company was buried in a chocolate-covered coffin.

GRIM REMINDER AWARDS:
IN CASE ANYONE FORGOT THAT THE END IS NEAR

★ **Third Place:** Buried Alive

The possibility of people being buried before they were totally dead became such an obsession in Victorian England that a watchdog group was formed called the Society for the Prevention of People Being Buried Alive.

Under the society's paranoid hectoring, it became the English custom to leave dead people lying in the parlor for a week or two before burying them.

The limit was reached when the duke of Wellington died in 1852 but wasn't buried until two months later. By that time, they were pretty sure he was gone.

★ **Runner-up:** The Long Cemetery

Remember the Oregon Trail that the pioneers followed west? A rough road. On average there's a grave marking a fallen pioneer for every eighty yards of the trail—or twenty-two graves per mile.

★ **And the Winner Is:** The Temporary Shortstop

Which position on a baseball team should you play if you want to live longer? And which position should you avoid because it has the shortest life span?

The Metropolitan Life Insurance Company's researchers determined statistically that third basemen live longer than other players. But don't be a shortstop. Their lives end sooner than any of the other starting nine.

THE FASHIONABLY DEAD PRIZE:
FOR THE CLOTHING SUPERSTITION
THAT EVERYONE LOOKS GOOD IN BLACK

People who've lost a loved one wear black out of respect for the passages of the dead. But respect is not the origin of that custom—it's fear of the dead.

People felt that if a widow wore black, the spirit of her dead husband wouldn't be able to see her and therefore would leave her alone.

THE HAIR TODAY, GONE TOMORROW PRIZE:
FOR POSTMORTEM TRIMS

★ **Third Place:** Haircut Number One

In ancient times people saved the hair they cut and teeth they lost for the rest of their lives. The extras would then be buried with the person so he would be complete on the other side.

★ **Runner-up:** Haircut Number Two

In his will Napoleon left his hair—to be cut off his dead body and divided among his friends.

★ **And the Winner Is:** Haircut Number Three

When his wife died in 1872, Benjamin Disraeli (who had served as England's prime minister) found out she had saved all of his hair, which she'd cut since they had gotten married thirty-two years previously.

GRAVE AWARDS: FOR INSULTS THAT DON'T STOP JUST BECAUSE THE VICTIM IS DECEASED

★ Third Place: Ex-Sisters

Joan Fontaine and Olivia de Havilland were sisters who both became movie stars, but feuded their entire careers. It was all a matter of jealousy, according to Joan: "I married first, won the Oscar before Olivia did; and if I die first, she'll undoubtedly be livid because I beat her to it."

★ Runner-up: On Cue

Movie star Tallulah Bankhead thought rival star Pola Negri was hamming it up at the funeral of matinee idol Rudolph Valentino. Bankhead accused Negri of pretending that she and Valentino had been in love to get publicity.

"She fainted at the funeral," Tallulah said, "not just once but on request."

★ And the Winner Is: One Last Role

Actress Elsa Lanchester, speaking about other actresses who continue to work in films into their seventies: "I hope I never live so long that I get hired simply for not being a corpse."

THE EX-EXECUTIVE PRIZE: FOR THE INCONVENIENT BUSINESS OF DYING

Businesswoman Elizabeth Arden ran her cosmetics firm until she died at the age of eighty-seven. Surprised to find that such an energetic woman had finally passed, one of her employees exclaimed, "But it's so unlike her."

THE MOTH AWARD

Centuries ago, people believed that moths were the ghosts of the departed, dearly and otherwise, trying to get back inside the house. That's why moths rammed themselves into windows.

THE LEGACY PRIZE:
FOR STRANGE THINGS PEOPLE LEFT BEHIND

★ **Third Place:** The W. C. Fields Memorial Orphanage
Comedian W. C. Fields left money to start an orphanage where "no religion of any sort is to be preached."

But after all his heirs finished fighting over and dividing up the movie star's money, there wasn't enough money left to support an orphan, much less start an orphanage.

★ **Runner-up:** The Memorial Children
A rich Canadian lawyer named Charles Millar died in 1928, leaving behind a fortune to go to the woman from Toronto who gave birth to the most children in the decade following his death.

A court upheld the legacy, and the baby race was on. Ten years later, four mothers (with nine children apiece) split the prize.

★ **And the Winner Is:** The Philosopher
German philosopher Georg Hegel left the world with these curious last words: "Only one man ever understood me, and even he didn't understand me."

THE UNOBVIOUS DEATH PRIZE:
FOR ODD WAYS OF LOOKING AT THE END

★ **Third Place:** The Catch

In his darkly comic novel *Catch-22*, Joseph Heller wrote: "He had decided to live for ever or die in the attempt."

★ **Runner-up:** Bad Publicity

"All publicity is good," Irish playwright Brendan Behan said, "except an obituary notice."

★ **And the Winner Is:** The Escape

Writer Alice Ellis observed that "death is the last enemy. Once we've got past that, I think everything will be all right."

THE SO GREAT, TOO LATE PRIZE:
FOR SECRET POETS WHOSE WORK WAS
UNKNOWN UNTIL AFTER THEIR DEATHS

★ **Third Place:** John Donne

The part-time poet kept most of his poetry secret so it didn't interfere with his career advancement within the church.

★ **Runner-up:** Andrew Marvell

The politician's poems, including the now-famous "To His Coy Mistress," were published after his death by his housekeeper.

★ **And the Winner Is:** Emily Dickinson

Now recognized as one of history's greatest poets, Dickinson had only four of her poems published during her life. After the reclusive author died, her sister discovered a locked box containing a thousand of Emily's poems and the publishing feast began.

Chapter 22

Winners of the Animal Talent Show

The Society for the Protection of Slow Animals with Dull Teeth presents the All-Species Talent Show Winners:

MOST ROMANTIC DUET

The male anglerfish bites the female of his choice, then hangs on for the rest of his life. The two eventually join bodies and arteries so they can share blood and food.

BEST JESUS IMPERSONATION

The water shrew can actually walk on water because its feet contain air pockets.

Best Mini–John Goodman Impersonation

The water shrew again, for eating its own weight in food every day. But then, unlike John Goodman, it only weighs a couple ounces.

Most Likely to Succeed

Roundworms attach themselves to shrimp, turning them blue, which makes the shrimp more visible to ducks. When a duck eats a blue shrimp, the roundworm gets inside the duck's intestines, which is where it wanted to go all along to set up its new home.

Best Fake-out

To protect its ground nest, the plover distracts a predator by pretending to have a broken wing. This convinces the hunter that the plover can be caught, and the bird leads it away from the nest, then flies off to escape.

Marathon Chicken Champion

In 1945 Mike the Headless Chicken of Fruita, Colorado, defied a farmer's Sunday dinner by surviving for four years without a head. Only certain human politicians have beaten that record.

Most Talented Feet

If you were a butterfly, you too would taste with your feet.

BEST ASS

In a nineteenth-century gold rush, a miner's donkey got loose. When prospectors caught up to the stray outside the town of Kellog, Idaho, the donkey was standing on an outcropping of silver and lead that turned out to be worth $100 million.

BEST USE OF AN ASS'S EARS IN FASHION

King Midas, who got into much trouble turning everything into gold (including his dinner and his daughter), didn't do much better when he tried to rig a music contest.

To teach him a lesson, the gods turned the king's ears into an ass's ears. To hide his shame, Midas wore a tall, peaked cap.

The stylish people of Midas's kingdom thought the king was a fashionista, so they took to wearing the same kind of silly cap, proving that even though they didn't have ass's ears they did have ass's brains.

BEST BRAIN

Leaf-cutter ants have such a highly developed society that they easily adapt where humans cannot. People may never get along with each other, but ants will. They've learned how to cooperate to survive—something New Yorkers are never likely to grasp.

The ants divide themselves up into queen, attendants, nursemaids, builders, soldiers, food gatherers, and food processors—all without the help of supervisors, managers, or a CEO telling everyone what to do. And they've been doing it for millions of years, getting along just fine.

GREAT MOMENTS FOR ANIMALS THAT COULD KICK OUR BUTT

We put ourselves at the top of the tough guy chain because we're the ones who keep the list. But nobody keeps the championship belt for long.

Despite all our guns and bug sprays, there are plenty of species lining up to knock off the champ. Here are some of the likely contenders to kick the stuffing out of the human race.

1. Mosquitoes—These fearless people hunters kill millions with their arsenal of malaria, yellow fever, encephalitis, denge fever, and other deadly diseases.

2. Fire ants—You'd want to stay on the good side of the fire ants—if they had a good side.

Fire ants will attack newborn fawns with tiny ant fangs. When a fawn licks off the ants to get rid of them, some of them get swallowed live and continue to bite the fawn from inside its stomach.

If you think too bad for them, I'm not a fawn, consider this: fire ants will relentlessly bite people who can't get out of their path or smack them off, like the paralyzed and the bedridden. These ants have been known to invade homes and chew the insulation off electrical wires.

One further warning: they're multiplying. People who have wanted to look have found up to four-hundred mounds of fire ants in an acre of Texas farmland.

3. Poison frogs—In South American jungles there's a frog whose poison is so deadly one ten-thousandth of a gram can kill a person.

If their poison wasn't dangerous enough when wielded by the frog, Indians dip their arrows and blow darts in the venom and use it to kill their enemies.

From the frog's point of view, the Indians are just another method of spreading the frog's poison.

TOUGHEST NERD

Slugs seem like such pushovers. But just like men, they will fight to the death over territory or food—slashing, biting, and destroying other slugs with their vicious jaws and poisonous slime.

MOST MACHO

Men will be men no matter what species. Before a male dragonfly mates, he cleans out sperm deposited in the female by previous male dragonflies so that the eggs she lays will be his.

After mating, Type A male dragonflies will fly around attached to the female, to prevent other males from doing to his sperm what he just did to others.

Trickiest

Some spiders can imitate the scent of pheromones that female moths send out to signal male moths that it's time to mate. A male moth shows up for a date, but it turns out he'll be staying for dinner instead.

Whiniest

When chicks inside turkey eggs are ready to hatch in the nest, they start peeping—the fowl version of whining. If they don't peep or peep in an unconvincing turkey fashion, the mother turkey will destroy the egg before it hatches, assuming it's a foreign egg that doesn't belong in her nest.

Top Surfer

The bat flea doesn't jump to get on board his host, like the dog and cat fleas we know too well. These fleas hitch a ride up to the bat on the back of earwigs, who are headed that way with parasitic desires of their own. Dozens of fleas may ride an earwig bus at the same time, paying no fare at all.

Toughest Vegetarians

Milkweed is poisonous to most insects and birds. But not to the monarch butterfly, which dines on milkweed that would kill other animals.

The monarch absorbs the milkweed poison, which becomes its main protection. The same animals that won't eat the weed also won't eat the butterflies.

BEST TRAPPER

The Costa Rican assassin bug will kill a termite, then use the corpse to attract other termites.

Termites are tidier than their reputation would have us believe. When a termite corpse is located, other termites come scooting out of the nest to clean up the debris, only to become the assassin bug's next victims.

BEST USE OF GIRAFFES

African starlings live on giraffes, feeding off the ticks and fleas that also live on the giraffe. The starlings even use the giraffe as a mating bed.

BEST USE OF NATURE'S ROLAIDS

African termites grow a fungus within their nests that digests the food for them that the termites can't digest themselves.

BEST USE OF THE FAKE-OUT

The Indian Ocean crab has weak pincers, too weak to fight off its enemies. So the crab arms itself by attaching a couple of anemones to its claws. The anemone stingers keep away predators from the united crab–anemone front.

Hottest Salamander Dude

Rich salamanders, like rich humans, score more. If a male salamander is a good termite hunter, it shows up in his dung, which he piles up outside his hole-in-the-ground bachelor pad.

Female salamanders come around and inspect the richness of each dung pile. When they find a guy who's got the good termites, he gets the babes.

Best Moocher

You've probably known guys like the male hanging fly. He courts females by offering them food.

But a rival male fly may pretend to be a hanging fly babe so the guy with the food offers it to him. If the female impersonator gets away with this pretense, he grabs the food and flies off to find a girl of his own.

Best Speed Dater

The African hammerhead bat would do really well in singles bars. The male bats hang out in trees, forming a mile-long gamut, where they show off their studliness by honking.

A female bat flies along the gamut, inspecting the males one at a time before choosing the one she wants to mate with.

If you think we're so much more evolved than bats, consider this: the male bat who honks the loudest gets the most women.

Most Likely to Get Nicknamed Tiny

The blue whale weighs as much as thirty elephants and is longer than three Greyhound buses.

BEST MULTITASKER

Reef worms in the South Pacific live in burrows among the coral reefs. They stay so busy feeding on polyps that they're too preoccupied to have sex with other reef worms.

Fortunately for the future of reef worms, they have developed an unusual method of having sex without bothering to show up.

A multitasking reef worm pushes its back half out of its tunnel and breaks it off. The bottoms of two reef worms then get together to mate, while the worms themselves never have to leave their burrow cubicles.

MOST TALENTED FISH
(OR IF HE'S NOT, WHO'S GOING TO TELL HIM?)

The shark is the only fish that can blink with both eyes at the same time.

BEST USE OF SCARE TACTICS
TO MAKE PEOPLE SCREAM

The spider scares far more people than it will ever kill or even seriously damage. You are more likely to be killed by a popped champagne cork than a poisonous spider. Yet no one jumps on top of a table screaming, "Yewwww, champagne cork!"

BEST IMITATION OF A TEENAGER

The goldfish has a memory span of three seconds.

Best Mike Tyson Imitation

The roadrunner fights rattlesnakes with its wings and can swallow the snake whole.

Most Artistic, Heavyweight Division

When Phoenix zookeepers noticed that Ruby the elephant liked to brush dirt with a tree branch held in her trunk, they gave her paints and a giant paintbrush.

Ruby's paintings sold for thousands, which is better than most human artists ever do.

Best Long Shot

The red crab of the Indian Ocean plays the numbers game. A crab may lay a million eggs during her ten-year life span, should she be lucky enough to survive that long.

How many of those eggs will survive the rigors of young crab hatchlings as they try to avoid being eaten by predators or carried out to sea when they're still too young to fight the tides?

Two out of a million is considered pretty good odds for the red crab.

Best Junior Racer

An opossum mother gives birth to a lot of babies at one time, up to twenty of them. But she will have nipples to nurse only thirteen. As soon as they are born, the babes race into the mother's pouch and secure one of those nipples. The first thirteen finishers survive. The rest die.

Chapter 23

Champion Scoffers, Scorners, Insulters, and Other All-Star Wise Guys

"Things are going to get a lot worse before they get worse," said Lily Tomlin, back when she was searching for signs of intelligent life in the universe.

Whether she will eventually find them or not, you can enjoy the mind games played by these champs of wit.

CHAMPION SCOFFERS

1. German poet Heinrich Heine—"One should forgive one's enemies, but not before they are hanged."

2. Physicist G. C. Lichtenberg—"He who is in love with himself has at least this advantage: he won't encounter many rivals."

3. Benjamin Franklin—"A learned blockhead is a greater blockhead than an ignorant one."

4. Grumpy baseball slugger Ted Williams—"All managers are losers. They're the most expendable pieces of furniture on earth." (Williams stood by his call even after he became a manager.)

5. Moviemaker Woody Allen—"In Beverly Hills they don't throw their garbage away. They make it into television shows."

6. The Old Farmer's Almanac—"If Patrick Henry thought that taxation without representation was bad, he should see how bad it is with representation."

7. Naturalist Richard Conniff—"The working journalist should strive to be no more than half as dumb as a politician seeking office."

8. Screenwriter Ben Hecht—"In Hollywood a starlet is the name for any woman under thirty who is not actively employed in a brothel."

CHAMPION CYNICS

1. Irish playwright George Bernard Shaw—"The power of accurate observation is commonly called cynicism by those who have not got it."

2. Writer Ambrose Bierce—"A cynic is a blackguard whose faulty vision sees things as they are, not as they ought to be."

3. Writer Shirley Ann Grau—"Haven't you ever noticed how highways always get beautiful near the state capital?"

4. Writer H. L. Mencken—"A cynic is a man who, when he smells flowers, looks around for a coffin."

5. British writer Jerome K. Jerome—"It is always the best policy to tell the truth, unless, of course, you are an exceptionally good liar."

6. President Thomas Jefferson—"I tremble for my country when I reflect that God is just."

7. Cartoonist Jules Feiffer—"Getting out of bed in the morning is an act of false confidence."

8. Writer Don Marquis—"A pessimist is a person who has had to listen to too many optimists."

CHAMPION SCORNERS

1. Writer Albert Camus—"There is no fare that cannot be surmounted by scorn."

2. Irish playwright George Bernard Shaw—"The world is populated in the main by people who should not exist."

3. When Mark Twain got into an argument with a Mormon about polygamy, the Mormon demanded that Twain point out any passage in the Bible where the Mormon practice of taking more than one wife is actually forbidden.

Twain easily found one—"No man can serve two masters."

4. Poet Robert Frost—"A jury consists of twelve persons chosen to decide who has the better lawyer."

5. English writer Samuel Johnson—"Americans are a race of convicts and ought to be thankful for anything we allow them short of hanging."

6. Writer Don Marquis—"An optimist is a guy that has never had much experience."

7. Writer Mark Twain—"It could probably be shown by facts and figures that there is no distinctly native American criminal class except Congress."

8. Writer Ambrose Bierce—"A bore is a person who talks when you wish him to listen."

9. Poet Robert Frost—"A bank is a place where they lend you an umbrella in fair weather and ask for it back when it begins to rain."

10. Diplomat Henry Kissinger, on the perks of fame—"When I bore people at a party, they think it's their fault."

CHAMPION COUNTERPUNCHERS

1. Painter Georgia O'Keeffe wouldn't sign her paintings. When asked why not, she retorted, "Why don't you sign your face?"

2. W. S. Gilbert, the wordsmith half of Gilbert and Sullivan, criticized an actor during a rehearsal.

"I will not be bullied," the actor countered. "I know my lines."

"Possibly," Gilbert came back, "but you don't know mine."

3. Movie star Mae West was a notorious scene stealer. That upset costar Alison Skipworth, who objected, "I'll have you know I'm an actress."

"That's all right," the lollapalooza West said. "I'll keep your secret."

4. Czech foreign minister Jan Masaryk—"Dictators are rulers who always look good until the last ten minutes."

5. Writer Mark Twain—"All say how hard it is that we have to die. A strange complaint to come from the mouths of people who have had to live."

CHAMPION WISE GUYS

1. Diplomat Henry Kissinger—"The illegal we do immediately. The unconstitutional takes a little longer."

2. Writer Wynn Catlin—"Diplomacy is the art of saying, 'Nice doggie!' till you can find a rock."

3. Writer Mark Twain—"If you pick up a starving dog and make him prosperous, he will not bite you. This is the principal difference between a man and a dog."

4. Poet Carl Sandburg—"A politician should have three hats. One for throwing in the ring, one for talking through and one for pulling rabbits out of if elected."

5. Two-time unsuccessful presidential candidate Adlai Stevenson—"I am now seasoned enough to have learned that the hardest thing about any political campaign is how to win without proving that you are unworthy of winning."

6. English Prime Minister Winston Churchill—"Political ability is the ability to foretell what is going to happen tomorrow, next week, next month and next year—and to have the ability afterwards to explain why it didn't happen."

7. TV newsman David Brinkley—"The one function that TV news performs very well is that when there is no news we give it to you with the same emphasis as if there was news."

8. Writer Mark Twain—"Let us be thankful for the fools. But for them the rest of us could not succeed."

9. Writer John Updike, about doing too many interviews with journalists—"You say the same thing again and again, and when you do that happily you're well on the way to being a cretin. Or a politician."

CHAMPION INSULTERS

1. Divine, the 280-pound transvestite who starred in a number of John Waters's movies—"All my life I wanted to look like Elizabeth Taylor. Now I find that Liz is beginning to look like me."

2. Comic Mort Sahl, about Hollywood stars Dustin Hoffman and Elliott Gould—"If they had been my roommates in college, I couldn't have got them a date."

3. Director George Cukor, about working with actor Jack Lemmon—"He's not one of those actors who'll bore you to death discussing acting. He'd rather bore you to death discussing golf."

4. Director John Huston, filming a scene in *Key Largo* in which Edward G. Robinson took a bath, described his star as looking like—"a crustacean with its shell off."

5. Movie star Rock Hudson—"I did not give [TV star] Lee Majors his start in acting. You can't pin that one on me."

6. Movie star Vivien Leigh—"Jayne Mansfield is to Marilyn Monroe what Richard Nixon is to Eisenhower—a crummy imitation and would-be successor."

7. Movie director Bob Fosse on actress Kathryn Grayson—"Not only has she kept her lovely figure, she's added so much to it."

8. Movie actress Joan Blondell on the older Elvis—"He wound up looking on the outside like what he always was on the inside, an overrated slob."

9. Movie star Anne Baxter about fellow star Tallulah Bankhead—"a marvelous female impersonator."

10. Walking neurotic Oscar Levant on the svelte beauty Audrey Hepburn—"a walking X-ray."

11. Critic Clive James on movie star Marilyn Monroe—"She was good at playing abstract confusion in the same way a midget is good at being short."

12. Movie star Ava Gardner about costar Clark Gable—"He's the sort of guy if you say, 'Hi, Clark, how are you?' he's stuck for an answer."

13. Director John Huston on aging star Peter O'Toole—"He looks like he's walking around just to save funeral expenses."

Chapter 24

The Bug Behind the Throne
and Other Hi-Q Honors

You ever wake up and think, no way today could be as stupid as yesterday. Then you think, yeah, but will I be saying the same thing tomorrow?

Petty stupidities rush in to fill the empty spaces in our lives. Yet now and then, startling episodes of intelligence pop out to surprise us with Hi-Q Honors like these:

THE POWER BEHIND THE THRONE AWARD:
GOES TO THE SMART WORM

There is a tiny worm that lives inside the intestines of starlings. But newborn worms are kicked out of their comfy home with the bird's excretion. Luckily for the worm, that bird dung is then eaten by pill bugs, who thrive on the copper to be found inside.

Still the baby worms have to get from inside the pill bug to inside another bird or no more wormy babies. Luckily for the worms, starlings eat pill bugs. Unluckily for the worms, pill bugs can avoid starlings by keeping to dark places where the birds can't see them.

But if a pill bug gets infected with one of these bird-dung worms, the worm takes over control of the bug's steering wheel. The bug now moves out of the darkness and into the light, where the birds can see it, eat it, and provide the incubation ground for another round of mastermind worms.

Don't you wonder who might be steering you?

THE PRODIGY AWARD: GOES TO THE STATISTICAL KID

Mathematician Karl Pearson developed the science of statistics in the nineteenth century. At the age of three, he showed an early intellectual inclination when his mother told him to stop sucking his thumb or it would shrivel.

Since the boy always sucked the same thumb, he compared it to his unsucked thumb and pointed out that there was no difference in shape between the two.

THE PICKLE PRIZE:
FOR UNCOMMON SOLUTIONS
TO UNCOMMON PROBLEMS

★ **Third Place:** The Land Dispute

South African President Paul Kruger was asked by two brothers to settle a land dispute fairly.

"Let one brother divide the land," Kruger decided, "and let the other have first choice."

★ **Runner-up:** The Moral Dilemma

King Louis XIV of France found a way around a particularly grave situation. When the great French playwright Molière died, the archbishop of Paris wouldn't allow him to be buried in consecrated ground. Why? Because Molière had never repented. His sin? Being an actor.

King Louis, who loved Molière's theater whether it was sinful or not, solved the problem by ordering the gravediggers to dig the writer's grave twelve feet deep, four feet below the bishop's consecrated ground.

★ **And the Winner Is:** The Love Knot

Rock legend Jimi Hendrix found a direct solution to an age-old dilemma. When he based his band in San Francisco, Hendrix rented a three-story Victorian house in the Haight-Ashbury. Then he installed one girlfriend on the second floor and another on the third.

THE PICKLE PRIZE:
FOR UNCOMMON SOLUTIONS
TO COMMON PROBLEMS

★ **Third Place:** Saving Money

When Vice President John Nance Garner lost a $10 bet to a friend over a ballgame, the friend asked Garner to autograph the bill so he could have it framed as a souvenir for his grandson.

Garner immediately took back the $10 bill and wrote his friend a check instead.

★ **Runner-up:** Making Tough Choices

When millionaire C. K. Billings decided to build a mansion on a hill over the Hudson River, he found a unique way to determine the best path for his driveway, which would go up a hill.

He bought a cow, set up a stall at the top of the hill and had the cow taken to the bottom of the hill every day. The cow soon wore out a path to the top, finding the easiest way up the hill. Billings then had his driveway paved along the cow path.

★ **And the Winner Is:** Dealing with Your Own Neuroses

Charles Seymour, the eighteenth-century duke of Somerset, had a strong distaste for rubbing elbows with the lower, middle, or, for that matter, any classes.

To avoid having to stay at inns on his frequent journeys from his country house to London, the duke simply built houses along the road one-day's distance apart.

GREAT MOMENTS ON AN OCCASIONAL CLEAR DAY FOR THE HUMAN RACE

1. From the visionary poet Ezra Pound—"Genius is the capacity to see ten things where the ordinary man sees one."

2. From historian Thomas Babington Macaulay—"The maxim that people should not have a right till they are ready to exercise it properly is worthy of the fool in the old story who resolved not to go into the water till he had learned to swim."

3. From writer Catherine Aird—"If you can't be a good example, then you'll just have to be a horrible warning."

4. From filmmaker John Sayles—"You don't need to know the language to watch [foreign] TV. Stupidity is the universal language."

5. From writer Saul Bellow—"A state of dispersed attention seems to offer certain advantages. It may be compared to a sport like hang gliding. In distraction we are suspended, we hover, we reserve our opinions."

6. From animation film pioneer Walt Disney—"Dream, diversify and never miss an angle."

7. From playwright Samuel Beckett—"Ever tried. Ever failed. No matter. Try again. Fail again. Fail better."

8. From writer Charles Bukowski—"Almost everybody is born a genius and buried an idiot."

9. From General Dwight Eisenhower—"In preparing for battle, I have always found that plans are useless. But planning is indispensable."

10. From comic Sam Levenson—"It's so simple to be wise. Just think of something stupid to say and say the opposite."

11. Businessman J. C. Penney—"Give me a stock clerk with a goal and I'll give you a man who will make history. Give me a man with no goals and I'll give you a stock clerk."

12. Poet G. K. Chesterton—"I owe my success to having listened respectfully to the very best advice, and then going away and doing the exact opposite."

THE REALITY SLAP PRIZE:
FOR CUTTING THE POWERFUL DOWN TO SIZE

★ **Third Place:** The Senator

Writer Julia Ward Howe asked Massachusetts Senator Charles Sumner to help a friend of hers in need. The high-powered Sumner dismissed her request, explaining that he was too busy to "concern myself with individuals."

"That is quite remarkable," Howe answered humbly. "Even God hasn't reached that stage yet."

Sumner, restored to his proper place in the scheme of things, promptly offered whatever assistance he could provide.

★ **Runner-up:** The President

Theodore Roosevelt had wealth and power and the presidency. It was his habit to step outside the White House and contemplate the stars before heading off to sleep each night.

"I guess we are now small enough to go to bed," he would explain to his staff.

★ **And the Winner Is:** The Coach

University of Kentucky legendary basketball coach Adolph Rupp knew something about playing under pressure. That's why he refused to call off a team practice and give up the gym so famed pianist Artur Rubinstein could practice for his concert there later that night.

"He can play ten notes wrong tonight and no one will know the difference," the coach explained. "But if my team misses a single basket, the entire country will be asking why."

THE AWARD FOR INFORMATION FILED UNDER B FOR BUREAUCRACY AND CROSS-INDEXED UNDER MB FOR MORE BUREAUCRACY: GOES TO THE INSIDER

Senator Eugene McCarthy spent a long time in D.C. politics and learned, "The only thing that saves us from the bureaucracy is its inefficiency."

THE ILLUMINATION PRIZE: FOR EXPLAINING WHY SCIENTISTS RARELY GO INTO POLITICS

Physicist Carl Sagan pointed out that in science, "It often happens that scientists say, 'You know, that's a really good argument; my position is mistaken,' and then they actually change their minds and you never hear that old view from them again. They really do it. It doesn't happen as often as it should, because scientists are human and change is sometimes painful. But it happens every day. I cannot recall the last time something like that happened in politics or religion."

THE INSIGNIFICANT PRIZE:
FOR REMINDERS FROM THE UNIVERSE OF WHERE
WE FIT IN THE GRAND SCHEME OF THINGS

★ **Third Place:** Changing the World

Naturalist Charles Darwin: "It may be doubted whether there are other animals who have played so important a part in the history of the world."

Darwin wasn't referring to Englishmen, scientists, or even human beings. He was honoring the earthworm for making dirt, eating garbage, and plowing the Earth. Without worms the soil of this planet would be so hard we couldn't farm it.

★ **Runner-up:** Changing the Universe

If the history of the universe were a twenty-four-hour day, the Earth wouldn't even show up until after work. As for people, we arrive a few seconds before midnight.

We are clearly the afterthought of the universe. If God made the whole place just for us, he might have spent a little more time working on the details of us. God knows we could all be a good deal better than we are.

★ **And the Winner Is:** Changing Our Minds

If the Milky Way were a carnival, our solar system would be a small freak in the sideshow. Our entire solar system takes 230 million years to revolve around the center of the Milky Way, which means we are now back where we started during the age of the dinosaurs.

How big is the Milky Way? If the universe could fit inside your house, you'd need a microscope to find the Milky Way.

☆ PART TWO ☆

Chapter 25

The List Makers Support League Presents:
The Top Lists of the Year

This year the league honors one of our all-time favorites, the number three.

THREE TOP REASONS TO MOVE TO ALASKA NOW THAT WE CAN PRETTY MUCH FORGET ABOUT FINDING GOLD

1. Bragging rights. You could fit 2 Texases inside Alaska or 90 Hawaiis or 425 Rhode Islands.

2. You don't need to bring a flyswatter. Alaska is the only state in the union without flies. Too cold for them.

3. It's the cheapest state we ever bought. In 1867 the Russians sold us Alaska for 2 cents an acre. If we had bought Delaware at the same price, the entire state would have cost $49.78.

THREE FAMOUS PEOPLE WITH GREAT NICKNAMES

1. Baseball great Lou Gehrig—Piano Legs, Old Biscuit Pants.

2. The Sultan of Swat himself, Babe Ruth—Jidge, Big Bam, the Slambino, Bustin' Babe, the Caliph of Clout, the High Priest of Swat, the Wizard of Whack, the Behemoth of Blast, the Colossus of Clout, the Caliph of Crash, King of Diamonds, Bambustin' Babe, the Great Gate God.

3. Splatter painter Jackson Pollack—Jack the Dripper.

THREE DECADES OF BAD BANDS NAME

1. The Sixties—Friends of Distinction ("Grazing in the Grass"); The Swingin' Medallions ("Double Shot of My Baby's Love"); The Electric Prunes ("I Had Too Much to Dream Last Night").

2. The Seventies—100 Proof Aged in Soul ("Somebody's Been Sleeping"); Brenda and the Tabulations ("Right on the Tip of My Tongue"); Disco Tex and the Sex-o-Lettes ("I Wanna Dance wit' Choo").

3. The Eighties—Kajagoogoo ("Too Shy"); Spandau Ballet ("Gold"); A-ha ("Take on Me").

THREE EARLY STAND-UP COMEDIANS

1. Chris Rok, the first prehistoric stand-up—"So, folks, why did the chicken cross the road? How would I know? What's a road?"

2. Jokerian of Ancient Rome—"O mighty Emperor, you Brutus you. We who are about to salute you could die laughing. I mean, fight to the death? I don't think so. Where's the future in that? Hey, just ran into my friend Icarus. He told me, 'I just flew in from

Athens, and boy are my arms tired.' Whoa, put that spear down, big fella. You could hurt someone with that thing."

3. "And now let's welcome, all the way from Russia, Leo Tolstoy, the Russian Laugh Machine."

"Thank you, ladies and cossacks, it's great to be here tonight. Actually, considering the pogroms, it's great to be anywhere. But like I said to Count Vronsky, take my wife . . . please. And he did."

THREE HOLLYWOOD EFFORTS TO SHOW THAT MOVIE STUDIO MOGULS ARE PEOPLE TOO ONLY WITH BETTER PRODUCTION VALUES

1. The Take Your Chauffeur to Work Program.

2. The Millionaire Man March: a support group for Hollywood executives who love their kids so much they make sure that one of their secretaries never misses the kid's soccer games.

3. The in-studio ESP Café: you walk in and there's a table waiting for you. No reservations. We knew you'd be coming.

THE ROCKIN' DOCS THREE FAVORITE MEDICAL SONGS

1. "All of Me" ("You took the part that once was my heart, so why not take all of me?")

2. The Bee Gees' "How Can You Mend a Broken Heart?"

3. Tom Petty's "Waiting" ("And the waiting is the hardest part.")

THREE FAVORITE SONGS OF PSYCHIATRISTS

1. Tom Petty's "Breakdown" ("Break down, go ahead and give it to me . . . Break down, it's all right.")
2. The Fortunes—"You've Got Your Troubles, I've Got Mine."
3. Little Anthony and the Imperials—"(I Think I'm) Going Out of My Head."

THREE FAVORITE SONGS OF FOOTBALL PLAYERS

1. Glen Campbell's "Wichita Lineman."
2. Simon & Garfunkel's "I Am a Rock."
3. Elton John's "Bennie and the Jets."

THREE FAVORITE SONGS OF OPTOMETRISTS

1. Sheena Easton's "For Your Eyes Only."
2. England Dan and John Ford Coley's "I'd Really Love to See You Tonight."
3. Johnny Nash's "I Can See Clearly Now."

THREE ODD REASONS BASEBALL PLAYERS CHOSE THEIR UNIFORM NUMBERS

1. New York Giants pitcher Bill Voiselle wore number ninety-six. Voiselle, who won twenty-one games in 1944, came from a small South Carolina town with the unusual name of Ninety-six.
2. San Francisco Giants pitcher Shawn Estes wore number fifty-five. "My favorite number is five," he explained. "I thought two fives would be better than one. If they go to three digits, I'd become 555."

3. St. Louis Browns Edward Gaedel wore number ⅛. Gaedel, who stood three-feet-seven, was sent up to pinch hit by eccentric team owner Bill Veeck in 1951. It was Gaedel's only plate appearance, and he walked. That's better than most one-at-batters have done.

THREE ORDINARY THINGS MANY PEOPLE WISH THEY'D NEVER SAID

1. "I do."
2. "How much do you need?"
3. "Fast-food management trainee? That sounds like a job with a real future."

THREE WAYS TO GET OUT OF JURY DUTY

1. Wear sandals to court. It shows you're free-spirited, and lawyers don't like that. They're dressed in $1,000 suits, and they expect you to dress up too, just not as well.

2. Carry a John Grisham book with you. Lawyers don't want jurors who will try to outthink them. They've already got the judge for that.

3. Get a job as a social worker or humanities professor. Prosecutors don't want softhearted jurors who care about other people. This is a threat to the legal system as they know it.

THREE FAVORITE MOVIE LINES OF PROFESSIONALS

1. Optometrists' favorite line, from *Butch Cassidy and the Sundance Kid*, when Paul Newman says, "I have vision, and the rest of the world wears bifocals."

2. Lawyers' favorite line, from *Lifeboat*, when John Hodiak asks, "Whose law? We're on our own here. We can make our own law."

3. Professional wrestlers' favorite line, from *Harvey*, when Jimmy Stewart says, "I've wrestled with reality for thirty-five years, Doctor, and I'm happy to state I finally won out over it."

THREE THINGS THE CHINESE INVENTED THAT YOU PROBABLY DIDN'T KNOW THEY DID

1. The zoo in 1900 B.C. The first Chinese zoo was known as the Park of Intelligence.

2. The dictionary.

3. Overpopulation. The Chinese were already up to 57 million by the first century.

THREE FILMS IN WHICH COMIC ROBIN WILLIAMS GETS TRAPPED

1. In *Jumanji* Williams spends twenty-six years trapped inside a magic board game waiting to be freed with a roll of the dice.

2. In *Aladdin* he's a genie trapped in a bottle.

3. In *Mrs. Doubtfire* he's a man trapped in women's clothes.

Here's a weird bonus: In *Hook* Williams plays a boy trapped in the body of a middle-aged Peter Pan.

THREE INVENTIONS THAT DIDN'T QUITE BECOME AS BIG AS THEY THOUGHT THEY WOULD

1. When the X-ray machine was invented, a clever merchandising man immediately tried to sell prudish Victorians on the essential accessory, X-ray proof underwear.

2. Roller skates for horses in the 1930s.

3. In 1959 a Milwaukee woman invented bird diapers. Could have sold millions, but somehow the idea didn't catch on.

THREE SCENES REPUTEDLY FOUND ON SHAKESPEARE'S CUTTING-ROOM FLOOR

1. From *King Lear,* the idiot behind the throne—

Enter Lear's Chairman of the Kingdom Planning Commission. He speaks:

"A nice set of cookware is always a good gift, my liege. Daughters should like that. But if you must divide the kingdom, hang on to that summer castle. Just in case it doesn't work out with the girls. Those three are always squabbling over something."

2. From *Macbeth,* a servant's work is never done—

Enter Lady Macbeth, followed by the castle maid. She speaks:

"Look, Lady, I just put fresh sheets on all the beds in the guest wing, so I hope, you know, there's not going to be such a big mess like last time we had company. Those spots, not so easy to get out in the wash."

3. From *Hamlet,* pal, you really need to get some counseling—

Hamlet paces. The counselor from Elsinore Mediation Services speaks:

"Okay, Hamlet, I want you to take a deep breath. Maybe if you and your new father had more activities to share . . . Well, what do you like to do? Uh, huh, looking for ghosts, that can be rewarding. How about the two of you take in a play? Or go to a good sword fight together. The point is, Prince, he's family and he's going to be king for a long time. So can't everybody just get along?"

THREE PRODUCTS OF THE FUTURE

1. Killer cigarettes—the only brand with your fair share of tar and nicotine. And a little bit extra.

Let's clear the air. Yeah, right? If we wanted to clear the air, why would we be smoking?

Smoke Killers, the only honest cigarette, and take someone with you.

2. Heavy beer—for the way you really feel.

We put back in that .75 calorie that the lite beers take out. Then we toss in another 598 calories. Per swig. Just for the heck of it.

Heavy beer, because lite beers are for wimps.

3. Shoes for liberals—at last, you can walk a mile in their shoes because you're liberal, you care. With our prestressed, used and abused shoes, you can feel the pain, the pinched toes and the bunions of the common man—or common woman—your choice.

Before we sell any pair of Liberal Shoes, we have a genuine disadvantaged person wear them on his or her own miserable feet or foot. You can buy the shoes guilt-free, knowing that you are striding toe-to-toe with the poor and helping them find meaningful employment at the same time.

Also available: Conservative Shoes—a full two shoes in each pair, and both of them right.

THREE INSULTING TRIBUTES TO UNUSUAL PEOPLE

1. Wilcy Moore was the Yankees' best relief pitcher during the Babe Ruth era, but he was a terrible hitter. The Babe once bet Wilcy $300 that Moore wouldn't get three hits all season.

Moore won the bet with six hits. He used the money he won to buy a pair of mules for his farm. He named one mule Babe and the other mule Ruth.

2. Bill Peet, the cartoonist and writer, created some of the early animated masterpieces for the Disney Studio, movies such as *The Sword and the Stone* and *101 Dalmatians.*

While drawing *Peter Pan*, Peet got into a dispute with his boss, Walt Disney. So the artist drew the evil Captain Hook in Disney's likeness.

3. Sidney Story was a crusading New Orleans councilman in the 1890s. He tried to clean up the town's reputation as Sin City by moving all the prostitutes into one small part of town.

When the city council passed the law, that part of New Orleans where the oldest trade was plied became known as Storyville. Sidney was not amused.

THREE PEOPLE WHO WERE WILLING TO SPEAK THEIR MINDS ESPECIALLY IF IT WAS ABOUT SOMEONE ELSE

1. Two of the great American poets of the twentieth century—Robert Frost and Carl Sandburg—were contemporaries but not compatriots.

Said Frost of Sandburg, "Writing poetry the way Carl does is like playing tennis without a net."

2. Madison Lacy, who acted in the movie *The Wedding March,* recalled that it took director Erich von Stroheim fifteen hours to shoot one scene because "Von wanted Fay Wray to act, and that was a pretty difficult proposition."

3. Baseball exec Branch Rickey about fiery manager Leo Durocher—"He can take a bad situation and make it immediately worse."

THREE HISTORIC FALLACIES

1. Columbus discovered America.

Not. Obviously to anyone but a European, it had been here all along, occupied by people who weren't asking to be discovered and wouldn't have been cheated out of their land if they'd had better real estate agents.

2. The Puritans were pure.

They were party animals. Invented that whole bondage thing. Puritan women who were into it wore brightly colored identifying letters on their dresses so guys would know where to go for a date on Saturday night.

3. The meek shall inherit the earth.

Meek people have been buying this one for centuries without ever asking—When, exactly?

Perhaps when the unmeek have used up everything and trashed what's left, then are taken off to repeat the process on Mars, they'll donate New Jersey to the International Meek Fund, but under one condition—that the meek never give it back.

Odds are, when God said that the meek shall inherit the earth, it was a totally sarcastic remark that no one got.

THREE MADE-UP HOLIDAYS THAT ARE BETTER THAN SOME OF THE ONES WE CELEBRATE EVERY YEAR

1. Lampshade Day celebrates the English tradition of putting on the Americans. The English would have tourists believe they put aside a spring day to repair all the lampshades in the house after a hard winter.

2. Toast and Jelly Day, an annual homespun celebration for the folks of Lake Wobegon, spun by writer Garrison Keillor.

3. Maybe Tuesday, invented by writer Peter de Vries, in which quiz shows visit your house and take away prizes if you don't answer questions correctly.

THREE STUPID HOLIDAYS WE'LL HAVE IF THEY EVER PUT ME IN CHARGE

1. National Déjà-vu Day—On this holiday, whatever you had for breakfast yesterday, you have the same thing today. Wear the same clothes. Go to the same old job. Come home to the same people.

Oh wait, we've already got that one. It's called Tuesday.

2. National Yes-but Day—the day after Thanksgiving when we consider all the things we would be even more thankful for if they had gone just a little better.

"Thank you, Lord, for the food you put on the table, but did the turkey have to be quite so dry? And those rolls—good, but not burnt on the bottom would have been even better. While we're fixing things, not having Uncle Phil show up next year would make us that much more thankful."

3. National Odder Day—on this day I celebrate the tradition that there are still people in America odder than I am.

This year I'm celebrating the Man Will Never Fly Society, whose sensible motto is—"Birds fly. Men drink."

Last year I would have celebrated the Procrastinators Club, but I never quite got around to it.

THREE FAMOUS PEOPLE INSULT WAGNER'S MUSIC

1. Philosopher Friedrich Nietzsche—"Is Wagner actually a man? Is he not rather a disease? Everything he touches falls ill. He has made music sick."

2. Irish writer Oscar Wilde—"I like Wagner's music better than any other music. It is so loud that one can talk the whole time without people hearing what one says. That is a great advantage."

3. American writer Mark Twain—"Wagner's music is better than it sounds."

THREE FOOTBALL STATS YOU PROBABLY WON'T HEAR ON *MONDAY NIGHT FOOTBALL*

1. It's easier for your team to have an undefeated season than to play a single game in which you never have to punt.

2. You're more likely to shut out the opposition than to prevent the other team from intercepting one of your passes.

3. It's forty times easier to keep the other team from scoring a single touchdown than it is to play an entire game without committing a penalty.

THREE FOOTBALL TEAMS THAT BELIEVED IN RUNNING UP THE SCORE FOR THE GIPPER

1. How does a football game end up 179–0? Sign Kingfisher College to play the Oklahoma Sooners in 1917.

2. Back in 1916, Georgia Tech was a football powerhouse. Cumberland College could barely field a team. Yet the two teams met in a game so incredibly lopsided that when a Cumberland running back fumbled, a teammate refused to pounce on the loose ball.

"You pick it up," the other player reasoned, "you dropped it."

Final score: Tech 222, Cumberland 0. The game was called on account of pity in the third quarter.

3. The greatest college team in football history? Not Ohio State, not Nebraska, Florida, or UCLA. Try Yale.

In 1882 the Yale eleven were unbeaten, scoring 482 points while holding the opposition to 2 points—for the season.

Even better: In 1888 the Yalies went 14–0, scoring 698 points for the season. The opposition scored 0 points.

THREE ORIGINAL LAWSUITS WAITING FOR AN ATTORNEY WHO HAS RUN OUT OF PEOPLE TO SUE

1. Sue Major League baseball to get the double play declared illegal for discriminating against slow runners.

"Baseball has no right to discriminate against players because of race, color, or speed," a slow player could point out to the jury. "If I was faster, they wouldn't be able to double me up."

2. Sue book publishers claiming that their constant rejections cause writers serious psychological damage.

"How many of those rejection slips am I supposed to take?" a writer might argue in court. "And they keep pounding in the same point—your book doesn't meet our needs at this time. Their needs? What about my needs?"

3. Sue boxing glove manufacturers for not posting warning labels on the opponent's gloves.

"They should have warned me that his gloves could cause serious injury," a KO'd fighter can argue. "Something like, 'Your opponent's right hook is closer than it appears.' Knockout punches decrease my earning power. I'm not okay if I'm KO'd."

THREE BIG BUTT CONTROVERSIES

1. Rock 'n' roll tricks teenagers into eating too much. "Get fat" is the subliminal message in songs like "Sugar Shack" by Jimmy Gilmer and the Fireballs, "Candy Man" by Sammy Davis, Jr., and "American Pie" by Don McLean.

2. British lawmakers raised an international controversy over who has the bigger butts—American tourists or Victorian Brits.

Members of the House of Commons debated the need to refurbish London's West End theaters because seats built for the modest rumps of the Victorian era were no longer capable of accommodating large-butted American tourists.

Alternative legislation to change the shows in the West End to *My Unfair Lady*, *The Overproducers,* and *Fat Cats* was tabled.

3. With Extreme Dieting, you can lose weight as you eat your cake but don't have it too.

Eat all you want. Doughnuts by the dozen. Ice cream by the brick. Cakes, cookies, fries dipped in gravy. It doesn't matter. You won't put on a pound when you exercise while you eat.

Through our revolutionary and rotational diet plan, which is completely unlike the other 7,239 diet plans you've already tried, the calories never get a chance to settle into fat because we run them ragged all over your body.

Want to eat a pint of Ben & Jerry's Super Serious Fudge? No problem. Just run three four-minute miles while you eat and you won't gain an ounce.

Want that extra piece of Boston Clam Chowder Cream Pie? Go for it. Just finish it off with three-hundred sit-ups, two-hundred push-ups, and a dozen five-hundred-pound squats.

It's not how much you eat. It's how fast you run while you're eating it. So stay slim—eat at the gym.

THREE DUMB THINGS MOST PEOPLE DO EVERY DAY

1. Not being rich.

While it's true that money can't buy you happiness, it has done pretty well for rich people.

Unfortunately, many rich people are in actuality poor people with too much money. The type of person who can accumulate vast wealth isn't necessarily the kind who knows what to do with it.

But if you learn to spend it correctly, money can buy you so many toys that you won't notice how miserable you are.

2. Work for people who are rich.

The only way most rich bosses can enjoy their wealth is at your expense.

The head of your corporation may earn $25 million a year for once a month saying, "Yes, let's go ahead with that," and once a month saying, "No, let's hold off on that awhile." But he can't really enjoy his money unless you're not enjoying whatever pitiful amount he tosses you to come around each day and kowtow.

The only reason he got to be the boss is he has the talent to walk around the office looking like he can tell if you're screwing off, or thinking about screwing off, or had thoughts about screwing off some time in the past thirty days.

3. Turn on the TV.

It's been known for years that watching TV will make you dumber. New research indicates that each time you turn on a TV set, your IQ drops half a point. We used to know why this phenomenon occurs. But halfway through the experiment, we forgot.

THREE ATTEMPTS TO MAKE SENSE OF LIFE BY FINISHING THE PHRASE: "THE WORLD IS . . ."

1. English writer Aldous Huxley:
"another planet's hell."

2. Austrian journalist Karl Kraus:
"a prison in which solitary confinement is preferable."

3. American poet Edwin Arlington Robinson:
"a spiritual kindergarten where bewildered infants are trying to spell God with the wrong blocks."

Chapter 26

The Nobel Realistic Peace Prize and Other New Old Awards

Have you ever seen a Nobel or a Pulitzer prize? You think they make them at the same shop they make all those bowling trophies?

As for that Genius Award, hey, they ran out of geniuses years ago. Now it's just a Pretty Sharp Award for all the B+ people.

Year after year the same old people win the same old prizes. How nice for their résumés. For the rest of us—boring.

The elite meet to give each other awards for one simple reason: they've already got the tuxedos.

What they don't have are TV ratings. That's why the new Prize-Winning Committee for New Prize Winners will try out some hipper, hotter awards—as soon as they get them back from the trophy shop.

THE NOBEL PRIZE FOR FAIRY TALE ECONOMICS: WON BY PROFESSOR HOBERT T. HUMPHLY FOR HIS RESEARCH INTO THE CAUSES OF UNEMPLOYMENT AMONG PEOPLE WHO DON'T EXIST

Here are a few of Professor Humphly's findings, presented in his controversial report, "Hi ho ho ho, it's out of work we go":

Cutbacks are a sad reality of business. But downsizing is even tougher for people who work in the fields of unreality. The economic downturn hits hardest those who are forced out of their fairy tale existence to take jobs in the real world.

1. Rapunsel left her ivory tower and went to work as a management consultant, teaching stressed-out execs the importance of letting down their hair. Her seminar "Out of Our Hair" urged working women to stop men from climbing all over them as they ascend the ladder of success.

2. Thumbelina went to work for a major corporation, but was paid only 40 percent of what a man would make in the same job. The executive recruiter justified this sizism by claiming, "She's only 40 percent as big."

3. Pinocchio attempted a career in advertising as a copywriter for Little, White, and Lyes. But the agency had to let him go his second day on the job when Pinocchio could no longer fit his nose into the office.

4. Rumplestiltskin went to work for ABC dreaming up new daytime quiz shows. "Guess My Name" was one of his early efforts, followed by "Guess My Brother's Name," "Guess My Weight" and "Guess My IQ."

The network was about to let Rump go when he came up with the blockbuster hit "Straw Poll," a game in which contestants compete to see who can suck up the most Yoo-Hoo through a straw.

5. Beanstalk Jack's old nemesis, the Giant, had a hard time landing a job at first because he was cruel, ruthless, and destroyed everything in his path. Later, he did quite well in politics.

6. King Midas found that even in the real world he had a touch for smart money management. He went to work for a venture capital firm. "Everything I touch turns to a 28.7 per cent return on investment after taxes," he declared.

7. Raoul, the tailor who made the Emperor's new clothes, moved to Beverly Hills, where he opened a fashionable boutique called the Bare Minimum. Made a fortune by keeping prices high and spending absolutely nothing on raw materials.

THE HAMBURGER-HELPER SELF-HELP BOOK FEEL-GOOD PRIZE

A seven-way tie between these unforgettable books:

How to Improve Your Memory by Forgetting Things You Don't Need to Remember; Everything You Learned in School You Don't Need to Know; Global Slenderizing: You Can Lose Thirty Pounds and Make This World a Less-Crowded Place to Live In; If You Think You're Miserable Now, Just Wait Fifteen Minutes; Men Are from Mars, Women Are from Venus, Marriage Counselors Are from a Galaxy Far, Far Away; Life Is Like a Vacuum Cleaner: It Sucks and You End Up Full of Dirt; This Instant Is the First Instant of the First Day of the Rest of the Next Six Months.

THE PULITZER PRIZE FOR PEOPLE WHO MAKE A DIFFERENCE IN THE WORLD AND STILL LOOK MARVELOUS DOING IT: WON BY WOWW (THE WORLD ORGANIZATION OF WEALTHY WOMEN), A NEW FORCE IN THE POLITICAL ARENA

Upon accepting this award, WOWW President Muffy Dredworth granted this interview to Quesella Shrdlu, editor of the *New York Times Magazine: People Who Are Even Richer Than We Are.*

Quesella: Could you tell our readers exactly . . .

Muffy: Actually, Q., you'd never find us in anything called an arena. A political arena? I don't think so. Circles are strictly what we travel in.

Q: . . . exactly how WOWW got started?

M: We needed a theme for our annual charity ball. We had already saved the whales and said no to all the tackier drugs. And how many times can you feed the hungry?

Q: So you were in a rut?

M: A rut sounds suspiciously like something that leads to an arena. No, our problem was we had run out of oppressed minorities, until we realized that the rich are an oppressed minority.

Q: Oppressed by whom?

M: Think of it—who has ever held a fund-raiser for the very wealthy?

Q: No one?

M: Precisely. Let one little peasant get tortured in some dismal country that no one goes to and you'll have Oprah camped on your doorstep. But the wealthy can be abused by headwaiters in some of the most elite restaurants in Paris and no one says pooh.

Q: Did you have any trouble recruiting members?

M: We simply invited the entire A list. As you know, no one on the A list can say no to anyone else on the A list, which is how you get on the A list. That and a truly significant number of millions. Our real problem was this: who could we protest to? As a class, we already owned everything worth owning.

Q: This is a problem the downtrodden don't usually face.

M: I'm sure you're right. But what demands could one concede to for people who already have everything? Then we realized that people who protest don't actually expect anyone to do anything about the situation. They simply want to make a fashion statement, politically speaking.

Q: Does your group actually walk picket lines?

M: No, we have our chauffeurs circle the block while we wave our designer picket signs out the moon roof. I have a lovely little sign from Calvin Klein.

Q: What does it say?

M: IF FREEDOM IS AN OBSESSION, LET ME BE GUILTY. Babs has a Ralph Lauren: NOTHING COMES BETWEEN ME AND MY TAX SHELTERS. And Dede Pheedy has a rather stark Christian Dior number: IT'S ME. IT'S NOW. IT'S EQUAL RIGHTS.

Q: We understand WOWW was organized by women for women. Why no men?

M: The men couldn't organize anything more complex than a corporation. But we've had years of experience putting together the really difficult events, like dinner parties and divorces.

Q: But you do let men into the group, don't you?

M: At first, the husbands pretended they didn't want to join WOWW. They thought it would interfere with grinding small companies into modest-sized smithereens. But they came around when we pointed out that anything good for the rich was good for business.

Q: What political positions has WOWW taken?

M: We were going to hold a sit-in to protest the war, but we couldn't decide which war to protest. We own so much of the world that we didn't want to offend any of our members who might be spatting. Then we couldn't decide where to hold the sit-in. One group favored Babs's condo in the Hamptons, while the other side was just as adamant about using Phoebe's sweet little villa in the south of France. Finally, instead of a sit-in, we decided to send flowers. I picked out the carnations for Afghanistan myself.

Q: Then you're neutral on international affairs?

M: Not at all. For example, we demand the U.S. get out of Monte Carlo.

Q: I wasn't aware we were in Monte Carlo.

M: Simply everywhere. The casinos, the resorts, the better beaches. And in such a brutal way, a veritable army of American tourists in their polyester dinner jackets and last year's bikinis. It's a crime against humanity, visually speaking.

Q: Then WOWW is not afraid to take a controversial stand?

M: Not at all. For example, we were against the nuclear test ban treaty because of what the Russians did to those lovely Romanovs. But then Missy Peabody, who knows, said that if we go ahead and have the nuclear war the rich might get blown up along with the poor. Even in Palm Beach. If this rumor turns out to be true, we will reevaluate our position. Meanwhile, we're declaring Fifth Avenue, from Fifty-second Street up, a nuclear-free zone, and we expect all governments to respect our right to privacy.

Q: How do you stand on domestic issues?

M: I've always felt that if you have to stand on your domestics, you're just not communicating clearly.

Q: I mean political issues?

M: We're in favor of raising the minimum wage to $5.00, as long as it's understood that's also the maximum wage.

We're against nuclear energy, unless someone can do something new with those atomic plants. They look like a bad set from one of those trashy sci fi movies. We would prefer reactors more along the lines of the Trump Tower.

Q: Pollution?

M: In general, we're not in favor of destroying our natural resources, unless it can be done at night or while we're away on vacation.

Q: What's next for WOWW?

M: Our highest priority is to make sure that our man gets elected president.

Q: Which candidate are you supporting?

M: All of them. That's how we make sure our man gets elected.

THE NATIONAL BOOK AWARD FOR THE BOOK OF ADVICE MOST LIKELY TO CAUSE PEOPLE TO BUY OTHER ADVICE BOOKS: WON BY *HOW I TOOK ABSOLUTELY NOTHING AND TURNED IT INTO ANOTHER, DIFFERENT ABSOLUTELY NOTHING* BY DR. BUSINESS

Here are a few excerpts of his career advice:

Dear Dr. Business:
I want to go to business school, but my father wants me to run off and join a rock band. Who's right?

—Confused in Boston

Dear Confused:
The average business school graduate earns $80,000 a year (or $89.95 after taxes). The average rock star pays an accountant $80,000 a year to count the money he makes from a concert tour where business school graduates pay

$89.95 (or their year's earnings) to hear him sing songs about the plight of blue-collar workers. But business school does have one advantage—better groupies.

Dear Dr. B:

Last week I attended a meeting even though I had no idea what I was there for. After an hour, it turned out no one else had any idea why they were there either. We had all attended the wrong meeting. My question: should I tell my manager about this?

—Meethead, Dallas

Dear Meet:

Only if you know who your manager is. Studies show that people spend 65 percent of their time in business meetings trying to figure out why they're there. The other 35 percent of the time is spent arranging for the next meeting.

Dear Dr. B:

For the past twenty years, I've been investing my company's retirement fund in the stock market, and suddenly realized that I've lost $15 million. Am I doing something wrong?

—Worried in Seattle

Dear Worried:

No, sounds like you're doing slightly better than the average investor.

Dear Dr. B:

I find myself attracted to my secretary, but he's a man and I'm not. My problem is if I invite him to work late, am I being too forward? I don't want to leave my husband because he takes such good care of the house. But I can't keep my eyes off my assistant.

—Edwina, San Francisco

Dear Edwina:

Imagine that the situation was reversed. Now imagine that it was inverted. Dizzy yet? Perhaps you should take a lesson from the male executives who have been in your position and refused temptations, if you can find one.

THE NOBEL REALISTIC PEACE PRIZE: WON BY THE THINK TANK FOR POLITICIANS WHO AREN'T SETTING THEIR HOPES TOO HIGH, FOR THEIR WORK IN THE FIELD OF SEMIPEACE

In honor of the winners, peace has been scheduled for next Thursday between 3 and 3:12 A.M. when most people have other things to do.

While we're waiting for peace, let's take a look at suggestions from the cowinners, the Alliance of College Professors Who Want to Keep Getting Government Money and Not Have to Go Back to Actually Teaching Classes. These professors devised federal guidelines to prevent future presidents from starting wars with people who don't know they're supposed to lose.

1. Be more selective in your choice of enemies.

Want to become president so you can drop bombs on the annoying country of your choice? Go for it. The constitution will back you up with the right to do just about anything you can get away with.

But first, have an actual reason for invading another country. Two would be better. Reasons like, they're really ugly. Or, if they had as many long-range bombers as we do, we're pretty sure they'd do to us what we plan to do to them.

Reasons like, they were really evil in last summer's blockbuster will be considered valid by Congress only if your popularity ratings stay high enough to justify their continued support.

All we ask is, don't bomb all the annoying countries at the same time or we won't have anyone left to fill the field at the next Olympic Games.

2. Leave God a little more wiggle room to operate.

For example, if you're going to insist that inalienable rights are given to us by God, don't complain when they're taken away from us by God.

In a democracy we get to choose the people who will screw up our lives. In a monarchy the people who will screw up our lives are chosen by divine right, which proves that God has no better luck picking rulers than we do.

THE DÉJÀ-VU PULITZER PRIZE FOR REPEAT LITERATURE: WON BY THE EXPERIMENTAL NOVEL *SO GOOD THEY NAMED IT TWICE*

We have cut the winning book in half so we could reprint it here in half its entirety. If you wish to read the full winner, simply read this half over again a second time.

So Good They Named It Twice

Miou-Miou, the chichi French actress, had had all she could take of the strange events of the past eleven days.

Getting off Flight 22, Miou-Miou, who had just finished rerecording voice-overs for the animated version of the classic film *Gigi*, was met at Gate 33 by her agent, Dee Dee Ecceau.

"It's so strange," Miou-Miou said. "But my life has become too-too déjà vu. Everything I do, I feel I have already done."

"You too?" asked Dee Dee.

"Yes, it's too-too déjà vu," Miou-Miou said. "Everything I do, I feel I have already done. Like that. And last night I went to a movie revival. They were showing a double bill, *Reuben, Reuben* and *The Russians Are Coming, the Russians Are Coming.*"

"Seen it, seen it," Dee Dee said.

"Me too," Miou-Miou said, "twice. Then today I was reading in the trades . . ."

"*The Hollywood Reporter*?"

"Yes, and *Variety*, that they're making a sequel to *Tora, Tora, Tora.*"

"What's it called?"

"*Tora, Tora, Tora, Tora,*" Miou-Miou said. "Then on the plane for dinner, I had mahi-mahi with cucumber salad, steak tartar, and couscous. And for dessert . . ."

"Don't tell me," Dee Dee said, "bonbons and *baba au rhum* cake?"

"No, coconut pie and papayas," Miou-Miou corrected. "Exactly what I had yesterday."

"Naughty naughty," Dee Dee said as they left the Seattle airport. "But when we get to the set, we'll straighten it all out with your director, Martin Scorsese."

"Where's the film shooting?" Miou-Miou asked.

"In Walla Walla," Dee Dee said. "We'll be there in forty-four minutes."

Miou-Miou had signed to make the film version of William Faulkner's novel *Absalom, Absalom!* She was originally cast to play a Parisian can-can dancer in 1888 who uses tom-toms in her act, but they moved the story up to 1999 and changed her part to a go-go dancer who uses pom-poms.

As they drove down Highway 55, Dee Dee told Miou-Miou about the other actors signed for the movie: Brian Benben, who had just flown in from Baden-Baden to play her papa, and Za Za Gabor, returning from a vacation in Bora-Bora to play her mama.

"I'm not exactly gaga over the casting," the actress admitted. "It's so-so at best."

"Tsk-tsk," Dee Dee said. "Too late to change. And you must be nice to Za Za. She got bit by a tsetse fly and the doctors think she has a case of beriberi."

"I won't fuss," Miou-Miou promised, "as long as they don't use Rin Tin Tin to play my dog."

"There's some good news," Dee Dee offered. "We've secured rights to background music from B. B. King, Sha Na Na, and ZZ Top."

Miou-Miou nodded, lost in the whirlpool of ruminations known as double-think. She looked out the window at the rows of duplexes speeding by, and a line of poetry floated through her mind: "The tintinnabulation of the bells, bells bells." It was all so absurd, she could only laugh: ha, ha, ho, ho.

She shook herself out of the reverie and asked, "Is everything set in my dressing room?"

"I've stocked it with your favorite candies," Dee Dee said. "M&Ms and Jujubes, and plenty of cocoa."

"And the studio is happy with us?" Miou-Miou asked, hoping they would also cast her for the lead in remakes of *Rachel, Rachel* and *Mary, Mary*.

"MGM is positively gaga over you," Dee Dee assured her. "This is a win-win situation for all of us."

As they reached the set, Miou-Miou grew apprehensive when she saw the rest of the cast waiting: William Hurt, John Hurt, Mary Beth Hurt, and John Heard.

I must stop acting like a yo-yo, Miou-Miou thought, and work double-time to make this movie succeed. Quitting now would be a no-no.

"Just wish I could shake this sense of déjà vu," she said to Dee Dee. "But what can you do? As we say in France, *que sera sera.*"

Chapter 27

The Society to Make Sure We Haven't Forgotten About Anything Presents: Odd Acceptance Speeches from Even Odder Award Shows

FROM AN ACCEPTANCE SPEECH BY STATISTICAL THERAPIST JUAN X. TENN AFTER WINNING THE TWO PLUS TWO EQUALS WHATEVER WE WANT IT TO 6.7 OUNCE STATISTICAL HONORS CUP

My research shows that 32 percent of the people agree we should be able to use statistics to prove whatever we want to prove. And I can prove it.

Consider the Society of Statistical Therapists' Happiness Survey. We found that:

Thirty-five percent of the people feel unhappy some of the time.

Twenty-four percent feel unhappy some of the time, but a different some of the time than the first group.

Eighty-seven percent of the people who said they were happy immediately began to feel unhappy once they had taken the survey, feeling that they must be missing something the other people were getting.

Ninety-nine percent of the people are happy 5 percent of the time, most typically between 4:15 and 4:30 A.M. when they're asleep.

But we weren't satisfied with those results, so we probed deeper by designing a Statistical Analysis of Life as Viewed by People Who Have Actually Lived It.

We found these surprising beliefs from people just like you, except a little different:

Life is hell: 25 percent.

Life is heck: 35 percent.

Life is great: Mervin Poppens, 2521 Cypress Avenue, East Meadow, New York.

Life was pretty good last Tuesday. Wednesday was rough. Thursday? Missed it. Friday? See Thursday. Then on the weekend, life was good, bad, good, bad, good until I lost count. That brings us around to Monday—please, don't ask: 76 percent.

FROM BEV HILLS, LIFE-STYLISH EDITOR OF THE *LOS ANGELES TIMES*, WINNER OF THE AMERICAN INVESTIGATIVE FISH-WRAP AWARD: FOR THAT PAPER'S EXPOSÉ *HOLLYWOOD PANTS: THE TRUE STORY*

Ms. Hills read the banquet audience an excerpt from the paper's thirty-seven-part series:

Movie stars are just like you and me. They have their butlers put on their pants one leg at a time.

Or do they?

On any given workday, most Americans face a critical choice: do I wear the black pants with the gravy stain or the jeans with the hole in the knee?

The rest attend NYU and ponder: in the cosmic sense, that gravy stain is just a speck in an immense universe of stains. I might as well stay home in my boxers and watch bowling reruns on TV.

But for the truly big Hollywood megastars, it's not so simple. Let's take a look at Tom Mega trying to put on his pants.

SCRIPTWRITER: Enter Tom. He opens his pants closet, the blue one, not the black. He stares down an endless row of pants. He reaches for a hanger, then hesitates.

TOM: Why pants? Why me? I've got to find my motivation here or I'll never be really dressed.

DIRECTOR: Tom, Tom, they're not just pants. There's that whole history angle. Pants have been in your family for generations. Don't just put on the pants. Put yourself into them.

PRODUCER: We'll get Effects to rig it so Tom can put on both legs at the same time, because at his salary, that's $90,000 a leg.

STUDIO EXEC: Pants? I don't know. *The Man in the Gray Flannel Suit* never made dime one, and *Underwear II: The Movie* was a flop. Pants sound too risky.

STUDIO EXEC II: We've got to get Tom out of pants and into something new or he'll never dress in this town again.

AGENT: Mel does pants. Arnie? Pants. Even Julia wears the pants in her pictures. Tom, baby, I want you to think: caftans.

At this point, Tom Mega shuts the closet door, sits down in his boxer shorts, and watches bowling reruns on TV, which proves that the stars are like you and me after all.

The International Unhistory Prize:
Goes to Professor Spangler Brugh for
Research Demonstrating That Everything
We Thought We Knew Was Wrong

In his acceptance speech, the professor reminded us that those who do not learn from the past are condemned to repeat it.

Whereas those who do learn from the past are condemned to be totally frustrated by having to live in the same world with those who do not learn from the past.

This vicious cycle creates a mixed race of the stupid growing more confused as they are constantly nagged by the knowledgeably ticked off. The result: a world where no one has any idea where they're going since they're unclear about where they've been or why they should bother.

For example, weren't we all surprised when it turned out that Rome was built in a day?

Who would have guessed? Not us, obviously.

Rome looked so complicated on paper. Or it would have if they'd had paper back then.

That's why they got Rome up so fast, didn't have to spend five years filling out building permits.

Turned out it was the Barbarians who floated that slow-Rome rumor. The Barbarians were ticked because they couldn't build anything but mud in—oh, several—dark centuries.

Rome in a day? Sure thing, the Romans said, no problem. But let's not stand around talking about it. We'd like to knock off the empire by midday so we can get over to Greece by sundown and help them put up some really good-looking ruins.

By the way, I hope you all realize by now that you should always change horses in midstream.

By the time you get to midstream, the horse you rode in on has had it. He's pretty much good for nothing the rest of the way.

As for those birds, two birds in the bush are actually worth more than one in the hand. This should have been obvious to anyone who actually had a bird in the hand. Particularly a sharp-beaked bird who didn't want to be in that hand.

THE VINCE LOMBARDI MEMORIAL TOUGH GUYS WHO GOT GOING TROPHY: GIVEN EVERY HUNDRED YEARS TO THE WORLD LEADER WHO WOULD HAVE MADE A GREAT FOOTBALL COACH IF ONLY HE HADN'T GOTTEN SIDETRACKED CONQUERING THE WORLD

This century the award was won by Bill Gateson, a millionaire janitor at Microsoft, to honor the company's twenty undefeated seasons during which they not only crushed the opposition, they crushed the referees too. Here is an excerpt from Gateson's speech, which he let us have for only $50,000:

Say what you like about Attila the Hun, but there was a coach who knew how to win games. Caesar, Napoleon, solid on the offense, could take the other guy by surprise. Put them in the Big Ten and they'd rack up the V's.

My first choice for toughest team in the trenches? Have to take the Mongolian Horde. There was an army of nose tackles. When you said five more yards, they gave you five, and they didn't care whose butt they had to knock off to do it.

They say football prepares young men for war, but they have history backward. It's war that prepares big men for football.

What is history but a bunch of defensive ends who are willing to nail their butts to the line in the name of not letting the other guy march down the field?

History books are written by Monday morning quarterbacks, but history is made by the guys who hunker down the line.

The Horde, maybe they weren't the biggest or the dumbest players who ever knocked noses. But they were the biggest of the dumbest and the dumbest of the biggest.

From the acceptance speech at the Academy of Motion Sickness by filmmaker Spilosh Spielcus upon winning the Lifetime Achievement Award for Nonart

If movies were art, no one would go see them. The average film costs $48.5 million to make. No one gives an artist $48.5 million.

They may give that kind of money to an art dealer. But you can pretty much count on the artist getting the spaghetti dinner.

Know what real artists would do if anyone gave them $48.5 million to make a movie? They'd throw an incredible party.

Then when they came to a month later, they'd throw another party in case they missed anything during the first one.

When they woke up one morning and scraped together a few stray thousand dollars that fell behind the couch, they'd panic. That's when they'd make their movie.

This is not how Hollywood prefers to see movies made.

If movies are art, then who is the artist?

Not the writer, whose work will be rewritten by eleven other writers, the studio boss, the director, the star, the star's agent, the star's number-one lover, the star's number-two lover, the director's psychic, and probably the producer's limo driver on the way to the set first morning of the shoot.

Look at the writer's art this way: the guy who wrote *Rocky IV* made more money than the guy who wrote *Hamlet*.

Not the actors. As Hitchcock pointed out, actors are emotional paint. If they fail to nail it, you can fix it in the editing. If actors were artists, you wouldn't be able to fix what they do.

Besides, movie stars have more important things to worry about than art, like the quality of their body double's body.

Not the director, who is in charge only up until the final cut. If the studio execs don't like the way the director made the film, they can have someone else pull it apart and put it back together the way they want it. You can't do that with a Picasso. He did it himself.

What about the studio execs? How funny if the people in the Hollywood system accused of killing art were after all the artists.

But exec-auteurs don't have final control over the film. Who does? The test audience that is shown an early version, then interviewed about what they liked and didn't. Films are changed according to their collective reactions.

Who are these test audiences? Ordinary moviegoers chosen to match the studio's best guess as the most likely people to go see the movie.

Even indie filmmakers have test audiences: friends, family, and anyone they can cajole with beer and pizza to give notes.

Can you imagine what a test audience would have done to Picasso or James Joyce in their group effort to make art more accessible, more entertaining, more capable of selling popcorn and soda add-ons?

"Love your stuff, Pablo baby, but you've got to do something about that whacked-out face. We don't have faces like that in Topeka."

Which is why artists don't make movies and movies don't need artists.

THE GONG SHOW MEMORIAL AWARD FOR QUALITY TELEVISION: HONORS EFFORTS TO MAKE SURE AMERICA REMAINS THE ONLY SUPERSTATION POWER ON THE WORLD'S AIRWAVES

Accepting the award, Syd Glack, producer of the PBS documentary *Disney Has Cloned Shakespeare and Got Him Under Option,* remarked:

I'd like to thank all the little people without whom I wouldn't have known how big I really am. But I can't thank them because my writers are on strike for better swimming pools.

Instead, I'll show you a clip from our made-for-TV movie, the scene where the Bard gets a crash course in writing from a Hollywood producer working on a remake of *Romeo and Juliet.* Roll tape.

PRODUCER: These love-crossed stars, Willie baby, they'll be big.

SHAKESPEARE: That's star-crossed lovers.

PRODUCER: Whatever. Now take this Romeo character, you've got him saying, "Parking is such sweet sorrow . . ."

SHAKESPEARE: It's parting. Parting is such sweet sorrow, that I shall say good-bye till it be morrow.

PRODUCER: Don't think so. Around here, there's nothing sweeter than finding a parking spot. You want to talk sorrow? Try driving around the block twenty times until you find the right power place. Till it be morrow? What's a morrow, my man? No, Romey would say, "See ya, babe." And here, "She hangs upon the cheek of night . . ."

SHAKESPEARE: ". . . like a rich jewel in an Ethiop's ear; beauty too rich for use, for earth too dear."

PRODUCER: First thing, no Ethiops, whatever planet they're from. Don't have a sci fi budget. Besides, a real guy'd say, "Get a load of that babe."

SHAKESPEARE: And this? "See! How she leans her cheek upon her hand. O! that I were a glove upon that hand, that I might touch that cheek."

PRODUCER: We can work with that. "See! How she leans her cheek upon her hand. O! that I were a glove upon that hand, that I might not catch any socially transmitted diseases."

SHAKESPEARE: Perhaps I was wrong when I said, "Never was a story of more woe, than this of Juliet and her Romeo."

PRODUCER: You'll be okay, kid, once you learn to read the trades. Point is, if we gross what *American Pie* drew, watch out for *Juliet and Romeo II*.

THE SOCIETY FOR EQUAL UNRIGHTS
COUPLE OF THE YEAR AWARD:
PRESENTED TO ANDY DANA AND DANA ANDY
FOR INVENTING THE UNMARRIAGE CEREMONY

Since neither winner would appear on the stage with the other, the award was accepted by their divorce counselor, Dr. Dan, who said: Nearly half the married people in this country are suffering from hetero guilt because they can get married and their gay friends can't. The other half are suffering from common, old-fashioned guilt. But now everyone can show solidarity with the denied by getting unmarried.

At this unhitch ceremony, the unbride and ungroom get the chance to give back all those tacky presents they've been storing in the garage since they got hitched. Here come fourteen punch bowls. As they walk backward up the aisle, the noncouple throws rice at the people in the wedding party. See how they like it. But first, the now wiser bride gets to kiss off the groom.

> DEMINISTER: Do you take this man and give him back?
> UNBRIDE: You betcha.
> DEMINISTER: By the power uninvested in me by the sanctimonious, I now pronounce you two people all over again. You may unkiss the free woman.
> UNGROOM: Say, gorgeous, what are you doing after the ceremony?

THE NATIONAL TEACHERS DEFENSE ALLIANCE
KEEP THEM IN THEIR SEATS AWARD:
PRESENTED TO AMERICA'S SKATEBOARD MANUFACTURERS
FOR MAKING THEIR NEW BOARDS SUPERFAST AND
EVEN LESS SAFE THAN THE OLD ONES

Quoting from the award certificate:

Working together, we can divert the destructive impulses of teenage boys by making sure they spend a significant amount of their aggressive years in casts and on crutches. We will thereby reduce violent crime in the suburbs and keep teenagers in their seats in the classroom because they will be unable to stand on their own.